ONE BALL KNITS

Purses

20 Stylish Handbags Made with a Single Ball,
Skein, Hank, or Spool

Fatema, Khadija, and Hajera Habibur-Rahman

WATSON-GUPTILL PUBLICATIONS

NEW YORK

As always, our great appreciation to our respected mother and father, who raised us with much love, and to our beloved brother, Mustofa, who always has a special place in our hearts.

A special dedication, too, to our late paternal and maternal grandparents, all of whom made a large imprint on our lives, and to our dear Uncle Yusuf, whom we shall always warmly remember.

Text, project designs, and schematic illustrations © 2009 by Fatema Habibur-Rahman, Khadija Habibur-Rahman, and Hajera Habibur-Rahman

Photographs and color illustrations © 2009 by Watson-Guptill Publications

Published in the United States by Watson-Guptill Publications, an imprint of the Crown Publishing Group, a division of Random House, Inc., New York.
www.crownpublishing.com
www.watsonguptill.com

Library of Congress Control Number: 2008935970

ISBN-13: 978-0-8230-3323-2

Executive editor: Joy Aquilino
Editor: James Waller
Technical Editor: Wendy Preston
Copy Editor: Elaine Silverstein
Cover design by Abby Weintraub
Page design by 3&Co.
Illustrations by Carmen Galiano
Project photography by Tamara Staples
Additional photography (pages 3, 6, 8, 29) by Bill Milne

First printing 2009
Printed in China
1 2 3 4 5 6 7 8 9 / 17 16 15 14 13 12 11 10 09

ACKNOWLEDGMENTS

We are grateful to everyone at Watson-Guptill Publications who made this book possible. We thank our senior editor, Joy Aquilino, for all her insight and dedication in developing this book. Her suggestions have been an important contribution to our work. To our editor, James Waller, thank you for all your helpful advice when editing our manuscript. You made the task easy and it was a pleasure working with you. To our copyeditor, Elaine Silverstein, we appreciate all your comments. To Victoria Craven and Timothy Hsu, thank you for your indispensable critique and input. Many thanks to 3&Co. for the layout. Thanks also go to Tamara Staples, for the wonderful project photographs that capture our work so beautifully; to Wendy Preston for her keen technical editing; and to Carmen Galiano for her detailed and clear illustrations.

We are also grateful to the many companies who contributed the supplies we used to create the designs in this book. Their generous support is greatly appreciated. Individuals deserving special thanks are Tom Ware and Wendy Lacy, of BagWorks; Margery Winter and Deana Gavioli, of Berroco; Judy Wilson, Kathy Muhr, and Kim Schlager, of Brown Sheep Co.; Cari Clement and Nancy Gadue, of Caron Yarns; Kathleen Sams and Terri Geck, of Coats & Clark; Emre Koc and Amir Koc, of Feza Yarns; Linda McGehee, of Ghee's; Joyce Trimmings; Jules Kliot, of Lacis; Louet Yarns; Ketsia Poteau, of M&J Trimming; Cristina Hyde and Dana Keller, of Muench Yarns; Anissa Blackwell, of Prym USA Inc.; Josie Dolan, of S. R. Kertzer; Cheryl Schaefer and Laura Nelkin, of Schaefer Yarn Company; Doris Erb, of Spinrite LP; Jack Aberbook, of Sunbelt Fastener Co.; Dana Jones, of Tandy Leather Company; Tracy Robinson, of Tilli Tomas; and Jessica Valentine, of Westminster Fibers.

Much love and gratitude goes to our aunts and uncles: Uncle Abdul Quddus, Aunt Nooru, Aunt Hasnu, Uncle Moshiur Rahman, Uncle Motiur Rahman, and Uncle Lutfur Rahman. Mohammed Alam, Abdullah, and Aasiya, your love and care are constantly felt. And to dearest Durdana Aunty, Munira, Shabnam, and Zainab: We value all your lovely comments and appreciation of our work.

Photograph by Bill Milne

CONTENTS

INTRODUCTION

A handbag is a lady's best friend. When choosing a handbag, individuality is essential: You want to make sure you deliver the right statement for the moment. All three of us sisters can be *very* picky when it comes to our handbags, so designing these twenty unique purses, each made with only one ball of yarn, became an inspiring challenge that brought us to a new level of knitting. Each bag had to be up-to-date yet classical, stylish yet accommodating.

Those of you who like to change bags with the season will find a range of designs to suit your needs for spring, summer, fall, and winter. The projects are organized by season and, within each season, by required yardage. Many different techniques are used to create and embellish the purses, including short row knitting, circular knitting, beading, and felting. Some of the handbags have patch or inset pockets; others have hand-stitched leather panels, vibrant embroidery, or sturdy hardware—whatever was needed for the perfect look.

If you feel the need for a fresh new handbag with a real designer look, try knitting the Moccasin Bag, on page 102, or the Classic Satchel, on page 96. Looking for an eye-catching bag for your spring or summertime strolls? You'll find that several of the handbags fit the bill, including the tantalizing Summer Bright, on page 13, and the vibrant Citrus Slice, on page 45, which is perfect for a walk down the boardwalk. For formal fall and winter occasions, there are alluring clutches, such as the Red Diamond Clutch, on page 108. For casual activities, totes like the Blue Spruce Tote, on page 88, will spruce up your style.

So pull out your balls of yarn. Soon you'll be walking around town with a unique bag over your shoulder or on your arm. There's no need to worry that your hand-knitted bag will look "homespun." Each of these purses looks as if there's a designer label hiding inside. No matter which handbag you choose, your friends will beg you to tell them where you bought it!

With all our best,

Fatema, Khadija, and Hajera

ONE BALL BASICS

YARN

Yarn is the essential element of any knitting project, and there are ever-increasing varieties available today. To help you figure out which one is right for your project, you'll need a basic understanding of the different types. Yarns are classified into three fiber categories: animal, plant, and synthetic. Animal fibers are derived from the coats of various animals, including sheep (wool), goats (mohair and cashmere), alpacas, rabbits, and even buffalo. Fibers in the plant category include cotton, linen, bamboo, soy, and cellulose-derived fibers such as viscose and rayon. Synthetic fibers, created from manmade materials, include acrylic, nylon, and polyester.

The majority of yarns you'll encounter are sold as hanks, balls, and skeins. Balls and skeins are ready to use as is, but hanks must be wound into balls before you knit. You can do this by hand or by using a ball winder and swift.

Hang on to the label (also called the ball band) that's wrapped around the yarn when you buy it. This lists the yarn's fiber content, the dye lot number, the length of the yarn in yards or meters, care and washing instructions, and any special processing done to the yarn. Most labels also provide the recommended knitting gauge (see page 12–13) for the yarn and the needle size needed to achieve it.

YARN WEIGHTS

In knitting terms, weight refers to the thickness of the yarn rather than to how much it tips the scale. The thicker the strand of yarn, the fewer stitches you'll knit to the inch; the thinner the strand, the more stitches to an inch. Yarn weights are divided into seven categories: Lace (33–40 stitches over 4 inches), Superfine (27–32 stitches), Fine (23–26 stitches), Light (21–24 stitches), Medium (16–20 stitches), Bulky (12–15 stitches), and Super Bulky (6–11 stitches).

Ball

Skein

Hank

Photographs by Bill Milne

YARN WEIGHT CATEGORIES

Types of yarn in category
Knit gauge range
(St st to 4 inches)
Recommended needle sizes

LACE

Fingering, 10-count crochet thread • 33–40 sts • #000–1/1.5–2.5mm

SUPER FINE

Sock, fingering, baby • 27–32 sts • #1–3/2.25–3.25mm

FINE

Sport, baby • 23–26 sts • #3–5/3.25–3.75mm

LIGHT

DK, light worsted • 21–24 sts • #5–7/3.75–4.5mm

MEDIUM

Worsted, afghan, aran • 16–20 sts • #7–9/4.5–5.5mm

BULKY

Chunky, craft, rug • 12–15 sts • #9–11/5.5–8mm

SUPER BULKY

Bulky, roving • 6–11 sts • #11 and larger/8mm and larger

DYE LOTS

Yarns are dyed in batches, called dye lots. Colors may vary slightly from dye lot to dye lot. To keep the shades in your garment or accessory consistent, you'll want to make certain that all the skeins you purchase for your project have the same dye lot number (you'll find this information on the yarn's ball band or label). Of course, for all the one-ball projects in this book, dye lot is not a problem.

PLY

Yarn is made by spinning fibers into single strands, or plies. These strands are then twisted together to create a plied yarn. The ply number on the label refers to the number of yarn strands that were twisted together in that particular ball or skein. Two-ply yarns are made by twisting two strands together, three-ply yarns by twisting three strands together, and so on.

STORAGE

Store your yarn as carefully as you would your clothing. Keep any unused balls, hanks, or skeins in a clean, dust-free area away from direct sunlight, which can cause colors to fade and fibers to break down. Plastic bins with lids, lidded baskets, or zippered canvas sweater bags are all good storage options. You can add cedar blocks or sachets filled with lavender or rosemary to keep moths away.

YARN SUBSTITUTION

The instructions for each of our designs list the specific yarn used in the project. This is the yarn we recommend you use. If you want to use a different yarn, you can do so, but knit a gauge swatch to make sure that the substitute yarn will actually match the gauge of the recommended yarn. You should knit a test swatch even if the substitute yarn is the same weight as the recommended yarn. For more information on gauge and how to knit a test swatch, see page 12–13.

GAUGE

The gauge measurements in our instructions refer to the number of rows and the number of stitches over 4 inches/10 centimeters of knitting. For detailed information about gauge, see page 12–13.

TOOLS

There are many knitting tools out there that are either essential to successful knitting or that will help make knitting an easier and more rewarding experience. As you develop your skills, you will find more and more ways to take advantage of the wide selection of knitting supplies and accessories available. Here are the tools that you will need for the projects in this book.

KNITTING NEEDLES

The knitting needle is your most essential tool. Needles come in a vast array of sizes and lengths and can be made from aluminum, wood, bamboo, or plastic, among other materials. For those who knit at night, there are needles with illuminated tips. If speed is your goal, nickel-plated needles may be the choice for you. Other knitters prefer the warm feel of wood or bamboo. It is important to pick the right type of needle for your project and one that suits your personal knitting style. Your needles should help, not hinder, your knitting efforts, so try various styles until you find the one that works best for you. Comfort and ease are essential when knitting.

CIRCULAR, DOUBLE-POINTED, AND SINGLE-POINTED NEEDLES

There are many varieties of needles to choose from, each with its own specific use.

Straight needles are the most familiar type; they are essentially long sticks with a point on one end and a knob at the other that keeps the stitches from sliding off the needle. They are sold in pairs in a variety of lengths, the most popular being 10 and 14 inches. A circular needle consists of two straight needles connected by a wire or tube. They also come in varying lengths. They are most often used for knitting hats, socks, and other items in the round, but many knitters also use them to knit flat pieces. Double-pointed needles are short needles with points on both ends. Sold in sets of four or five, they're most often used for small circular projects, turning sock heels, and making I-cord.

CABLE NEEDLES AND STITCH HOLDERS

Cable needles are short needles with points at both ends that are shaped either like a fishhook or the letter U to prevent stitches from slipping off the needle as you

KNITTING NEEDLE SIZE CHART

Metric Sizes	U.S. Sizes
2 mm	0
2.25 mm	1
2.75 mm	2
3.25 mm	3
3.5 mm	4
3.75 mm	5
4 mm	6
4.5 mm	7
5 mm	8
5.5 mm	9
6 mm	10
6.5 mm	10.5
8 mm	11
9 mm	13
10 mm	15
12.75 mm	17
15 mm	19
19 mm	35
25 mm	50

work a cable. When instructed, you will slip stitches onto the cable needle and hold them to the front or the back of the work as you knit the remaining stitches of the cable.

Stitch holders, which resemble long safety pins, are used to hold open neckline or other stitches that will be bound off or picked up later. They are available in a variety of sizes, but smaller ones are used most often.

STITCH MARKERS

Stitch markers are small plastic or rubber rings used to mark the beginning of a new round in circular knitting or to indicate where to increase, decrease, or change stitch patterns. When the instructions indicate the use of a stitch marker, slip the marker onto your right-hand needle and continue knitting as indicated in the pattern. Yarn shops carry a wide variety of stitch markers, but you can easily create your own by tying a contrasting piece of yarn around your needle at the same place you would position the stitch marker. When you reach the marker, slip it from the left to the right needle so it remains in place in the row or round.

ROW COUNTERS

Row counters are handy little gadgets that help keep track of how many rows of knitting

have been completed. Some slip onto knitting needles, while others are hand-held. Turn the knob (or click a button) to advance to the next number every time you complete a row.

POINT PROTECTORS

These little rubber or plastic caps slip over the points of your needles, protecting the tips and keeping stitches from sliding off. They also prevent the needle points from poking through the lining of your knitting bag.

TAPESTRY NEEDLES

These large-eyed needles with blunt or rounded tips are used for seaming, weaving in ends, and embroidering.

TAPE MEASURE

An accurate tape measure is essential for both construction and blocking. Choose a flexible plastic or fiberglass tape marked in both inches and centimeters to accurately measure stitch and gauge as well as the finished size of your garment pieces.

CROCHET HOOK

A crochet hook is perfect for picking up dropped stitches or attaching fringe. Smaller crochet hooks work better for these purposes.

PINS

Pins are used to hold and shape the knitted fabric pieces during blocking or to pin together pieces for seaming. Any pin will do, but specially designed blocking pins with long shanks and flat heads are both durable and easy to use.

BLOCKING BOARD

For blocking (see page 31), you'll need a flat, padded, and pinnable surface large enough to accommodate a fully flat and smoothed knitted piece. You can purchase a blocking board or simply use a folded towel spread out over a carpet.

SPRAY BOTTLE

If you use the wet blocking method (see page 31), you will need a spray bottle filled with water.

STEAM IRON OR STEAMER

Steam is required during the steam blocking process (see page 31); either an iron or a steamer will serve the purpose.

UNDERSTANDING KNITTING INSTRUCTIONS

Knitting instructions have their own vocabulary and terms that are important to understand before you start a project. Here are the knitting terms we use in our instructions.

SKILL LEVEL

We have divided our projects into four different skill levels: Beginner (first-time projects, simple stitches, and minimal shaping), Easy (simple stitches combined with easy stitch changes, color changes, and minimal shaping), Intermediate (a greater variety of stitches, including more complicated lace and cables, double-pointed knitting, color changes, and shaping), and Experienced (advanced knitting techniques, intricate cable and lace stitches, Fair Isle patterns, and shaping). Most of our projects fall under the Beginner and Easy skill levels, but if you're a beginner and feel that you can complete an Intermediate project, go for it.

FINISHED MEASUREMENTS

This refers to the finished dimensions of the knitted piece, after blocking and assembling.

YARN

This specifies the type of yarn used for the project and the approximate yardage included in the ball or skein.

MATERIALS

This list gives all the tools and supplies required to knit the project, including the materials we used to knit our samples.

GAUGE

Gauge refers to the number of stitches and rows per inch of knitting, based on the size of a knit stitch. The size of the stitch is determined by the yarn and needle size used, as well as by how a particular knitter holds the yarn. In our knitting instructions, gauge is measured over 4 inches/10 centimeters. If your gauge does not precisely match the gauge given in the instructions, the size of your finished piece will be different. It is therefore essential that you check your gauge by knitting a test swatch before starting each project.

Here's an example of how gauge will be stated in our instructions: 16 stitches = 4"/10cm over St st (knit one row, purl next row).

The Gauge Test Swatch
Even if you are using the exact yarn and needles recommended in the instructions, you'll

need to knit a test swatch to check the gauge. This is because not every knitter controls the yarn in exactly the same way, and you may get a different number of stitches per 4 inches than another knitter, even if you are both using the exact same yarn and needles. Using a yarn other than the one specified in the pattern will also affect gauge (see Yarn Substitution page 9).

To make the test swatch, use the same needles and yarn you plan to use for the project, cast on the number of stitches required to get at least 4 inches of knitting (usually 20 or more stitches) and knit until you have a swatch that measures at least 4 inches/10 centimeters (4"/10cm) square. Flatten the swatch, straighten the rows and stitches, lay the tape measure on top of the swatch, and count the number of stitches and rows as follows:

1. Count the number of stitches across 2"/5cm; multiply the results by 2 to get the number of stitches per 4"/10cm.

2. Count the number of rows along 2"/5cm; multiply the results by 2 to get the number of rows per 4"/10cm.

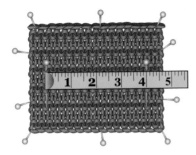

If you find that your gauge does not match the gauge given in the instructions, try changing your needle size. Larger-size needles will decrease the number of stitches per inch; smaller-size needles will increase the number of stitches per inch.

PATTERN NOTES

This section of the instructions explains any important information concerning the project, clarifications of certain instructions, or variations you might try.

COMMONLY USED ABBREVIATIONS

Abbreviations are used in written knitting instructions, and we provide a list of any special abbreviations used in each project's instructions, along with their meanings. To the right is a list of some of the most commonly used abbreviations.

*	repeat instructions after or between asterisks across a row or round, as instructed
( )	work instructions as a group a specified number of times
beg	beginning
BO	bind off
CO	cast on
cont	continue; continuing
dec	decrease; decreasing
dpn/dpns	double-pointed needle/needles
foll	follow, follows, following
inc	increase/ increasing
k	knit
K2tog	knit 2 together
LH	left-hand
p	purl
P2tog	purl 2 together
patt/patts	pattern/patterns
pm	place marker
psso	pass the slipped stitch over
rep	repeat
RH	right-hand
Rnd/rnd	round
RS	right side
Skp	slip one, knit one, pass the slipped stitch over
Sl	slip
Ssk	slip, slip, knit
st	stitch
St st	stockinette stitch
Tbl	through back loop
WS	wrong side
yo	yarn over

STITCH PATTERN(S)

In most cases, the stitch pattern or patterns used in a project will be presented both as written instructions and in chart form. You will refer to the written instructions and chart(s) when the project instructions call for that specific stitch pattern.

KNITTING INSTRUCTIONS

This is where the knitting instructions for each project begin. We tell you how many stitches to cast on, which stitch pattern to use, how much to knit, and how many stitches to bind off.

CHARTS

In most cases, the written instructions for each stitch pattern are accompanied by charts. These charts are visual representations of the stitch patterns. Many knitters find them easier to follow than the line-by-line written instructions.

How to Read Charts

Each small square, or block, in a chart represents one stitch or one knitting action, such as a knit stitch, an increase, or a decrease. Each chart is accompanied by a legend that explains the meaning of each symbol that appears in the blocks. You'll notice that there are numbers running along both the right- and left-hand sides of the chart. These refer to row numbers; for example, the number 1 refers to row 1. If the numbering begins on the right-hand side of chart, you will start knitting on the right side (RS) of the work. When the numbering begins on left-hand side of chart, you will begin knitting on the wrong side (WS).

Figure 1 shows a chart that begins with a right-side row. Notice that the numbering of rows starts on the right. This indicates that you will begin knitting Row 1 from the right, moving to the left. In this case you will read all odd-numbered rows from right to left and all even-numbered rows from left to right.

The chart in Figure 2 starts with a wrong-side row. In this case you will read all odd-numbered rows from left to right and all even numbered rows from right to left.

Figure 3 shows a chart as it will appear in the instructions, complete with stitch symbols. Each chart is accompanied by a legend for the symbols used in the chart, which corresponds to the written instructions.

Row 1 (RS): Skp *yo, k1, yo, k3tog, yo, k1; rep from * to last two sts, yo, k2tog.
Row 2: Purl.
Row 3: *K4, yo, skp; rep from * to last three sts, k3.
Row 4: Knit.

SCHEMATICS

Schematics are line illustrations that show the design, or design piece, laid flat. Schematics are labeled with the name of the piece and the exact measurements that each piece should be when completed.

Figure 1

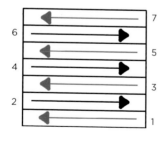

Figure 2

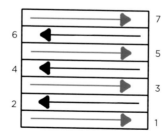

Figure 3

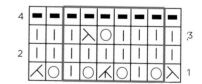

KNITTING TECHNIQUES

MAKING A SLIP KNOT

1. Pull out a length of yarn from the ball and form it into a pretzel as shown.

2. Insert the needle under the bar and pull a loop.

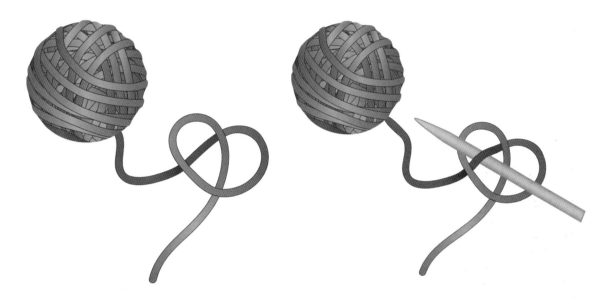

3. Tighten the loop with your thumb and index finger.

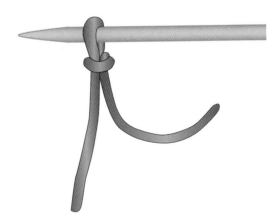

CONTINENTAL LONG-TAIL CAST-ON

1. With the slip knot on the needle, wrap the short end of the yarn around your thumb. Wrap the yarn from the ball around your index finger. Hold both ends of the yarn taut in the palm of your hand.

2. Insert the needle into the loop near the thumb and lift it.

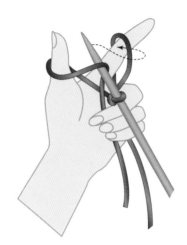

3. Keeping the thumb loop on the needle, slip the needle into the loop from the index finger.

   Pull a new loop through the thumb loop. One stitch is made.

CABLE CAST-ON

1. With the slip knot on the needle, insert the right-hand needle from the front to the back of the stitch. Wrap the yarn from back to front around the needle.

2. Pull the wrapped yarn through the stitch, being sure not to drop the worked stitch off the left-hand needle.

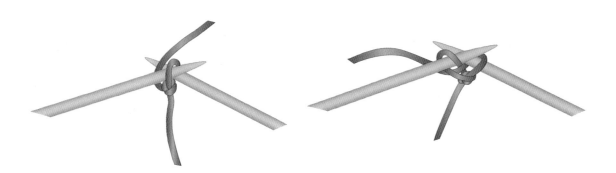

3. Slip the stitch from the right-hand needle to left-hand needle. Two stitches are on the left-hand needle.

KNIT STITCH

1. Keeping the yarn in back, insert the right-hand needle from the front into the back of the first stitch.

2. Wrap the yarn around the needle from back to front once.

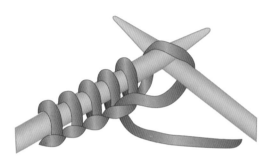

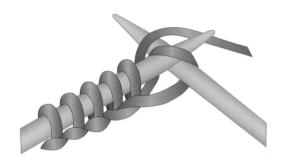

3. Pull the wrapped yarn through the first stitch.

4. Keep the new stitch on the right-hand needle; drop the first stitch from the left-hand needle.

Note: When every row is worked in the knit stitch, **garter stitch** is formed. Each ridge, or row of bumps, represents two rows worked. Garter stitch fabric is elastic and holds its shape well.

PURL STITCH

1. Keeping the yarn in front between the two needles, insert the right-hand needle from the back to the front of the first stitch on the left-hand needle. Wrap the yarn around the stitch on the right-hand needle from back to front once.

2. Pull the wrapped yarn through the back.

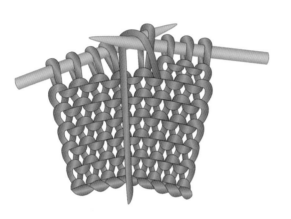

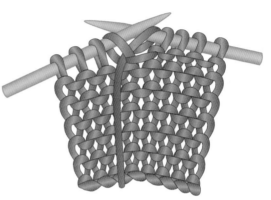

3. Keep the new stitch on the right-hand needle; drop the first stitch from the left-hand needle.

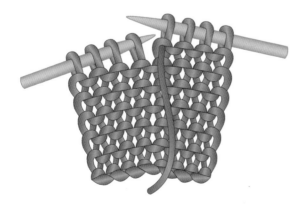

SLIP STITCH KNITWISE

Insert the right-hand needle through the stitch as if to knit. Slide the stitch off the left needle and onto the right needle without working the stitch.

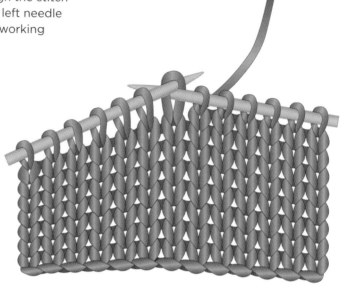

SLIP STITCH PURLWISE

Insert the right-hand needle through the stitch as if to purl. Slide the stitch off the left needle and onto the right needle without working the stitch. *Note:* The stitch will be twisted.

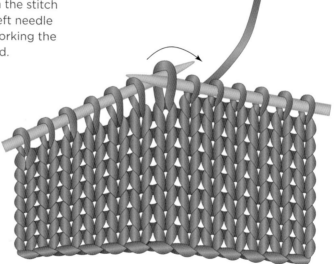

PICKING UP STITCHES

1. Working along the bound-off edge, insert the needle through the center of the first stitch. Wrap the yarn around the needle as if to knit.

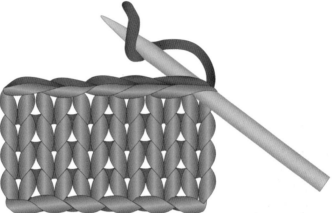

2. Pull the yarn through the stitch. You have picked up one stitch. Repeat to pick up additional stitches.

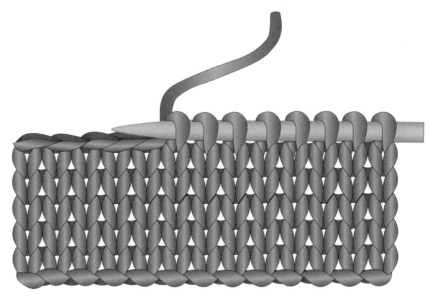

KNITTING I-CORD

Cast on the number of stitches directed in instructions. *Knit across the cast-on stitches. Without turning the work, slip the stitches back onto the left-hand needle; repeat from * until you have reached the desired length. Bind off.

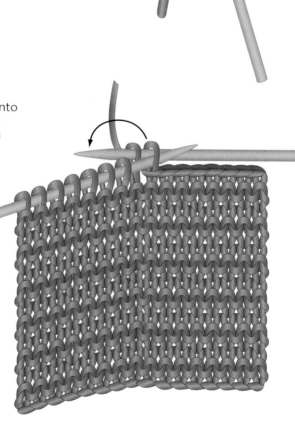

BINDING OFF

Knit 2 stitches. *Insert the left-hand needle into the first knit stitch on the right-hand needle. Lift this stitch over the second stitch and off the needle; repeat from * to the end.

THREE-NEEDLE BIND-OFF

Hold the two pieces to be joined with the right sides of the fabric facing each other and with both needles pointing to the right. Using a third needle of the same size, knit together the first stitch on each needle, as shown. *Work the next stitch on each needle in the same way. You now have two stitches on the right-hand needle. Lift the first stitch over the second stitch and off the needle. Repeat from * to the end.

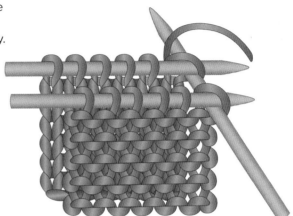

PICKING UP DROPPED STITCHES

Work to the dropped stitch. Using a small crochet hook, insert it into the dropped loop, hooking to the bar above it. Pull the bar through the dropped stitch. Continue to ladder upward by pulling the bar through the stitch below.

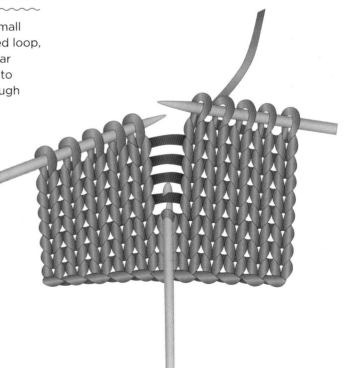

CIRCULAR KNITTING (KNITTING IN THE ROUND)

Cast on a number of stitches. Begin knitting across the stitches on the needle until you reach the last cast-on stitch. Work the last cast-on stitch, and place the marker on the right-hand needle point. Join the round, being careful not to twist the stitches on the needle. Tighten the stitch and proceed with working the next round.

KNITTING WITH DOUBLE-POINTED NEEDLES

1. Cast on a number of stitches on a single-pointed needle. Slip the cast-on stitches evenly onto three or four double-pointed needles.

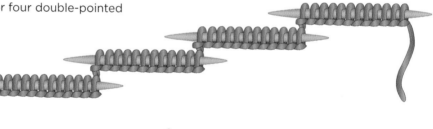

2. With the cast-on edges facing inward, take a free needle and knit the first cast-on stitch. Tighten the stitch and proceed to knit.

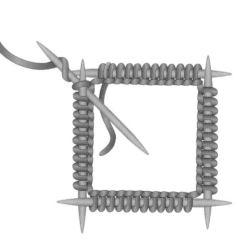

Photograph by Bill Milne

FINISHING

Properly finishing your project is as vital to a successful outcome as the actual knitting. In this section we give you instructions for seaming, blocking, and adding embellishments to your projects.

FELTING

Felting is a process that changes the texture, size, and feel of knitted fabric by altering the fibers so that you can no longer see the individual stitches and rows. It also shrinks the knitted fabric, but it is the fusion of the fibers, not the shrinking, that creates the felted surface. Any fabric made of animal fibers, such as wool, mohair, and cashmere, can be felted.

A fabric that has been felted is thicker, more velvety, and warmer than the original knitted fabric. Felted fabric can be cut and sewn because it won't unravel or lose stitches. Felting works particularly well for appliqués, hats, and bags. It's fun and easy to do, particularly when applied to fabrics knit with big needles (that is, with loose stitches). Felting projects usually instruct you to use needles two or more sizes larger than the yarn label recommends.

Felting is accomplished by subjecting the knitted piece to hot soapy water (which opens up the scales on wool fibers), then agitating the piece to cause the fibers to tangle together. When the piece cools and dries, the scales close up, locking the fiber into thick, durable fabric that won't unravel.

Felting can be done with a washing machine or by hand. *Note:* Make sure your knitted edges are finished, that the ends are woven in securely, and that all seams have been stitched before you begin the felting process. Otherwise, you'll create a big mess.

Machine Felting

Felting in the washing machine is the easiest and most reliable method. Place the knitted fabric in a washer using a small amount of hot water and small amount of laundry detergent (no bleach!). Machine wash the knitted fabric along with a denim garment (one that won't bleed) or inside a zipped pillowcase for seven to ten minutes. The denim (or pillowcase) creates extra friction, which speeds up the felting process. Check the fabric periodically, before you reach the spin cycle, to see if it has felted. You'll know it's ready when the knitted stitches and rows are no longer visible. Some yarns take longer to felt than others, so don't worry if your fabric hasn't felted within 10 minutes.

Just keep it in the wash cycle, repeating the cycle if necessary, and keep checking every few minutes. When the fabric reaches the desired appearance, machine rinse it in cool water and then spin on gentle (never wring the fabric). Remove the fabric from the washing machine (you will notice that it has shrunk significantly from its original size), lay it flat, and gently straighten and shape it, leaving it to air-dry. Remember that if you don't like your finished result, you can always felt it some more. (You can't, however, unfelt something that has already been felted.)

Hand Felting

Soak knitted fabric in a bowl, sink, or tub filled with hot water for 30 minutes. Add a small amount of laundry detergent to the water and hand wash it, rubbing the fabric together until you reach the desired degree of felting. Rinse the felted fabric under cold water to stop the felting process. Squeeze out the excess water (never wring), and then lay the fabric flat, shape it, and leave it out to air-dry.

BLOCKING

Blocking is an essential step. In blocking, the finished knit pieces are dampened or steamed and then smoothed into shape, ensuring that the exact measurements for the project are met and that all the rows and stitches are straight and even. There are two methods: wet blocking and steam blocking.

In *wet blocking*, the piece is laid flat, smoothed, straightened, and pinned down according to the project's finished measurements on a blocking pad or any padded surface. Once you are sure the rows and stitches are flat, even, and straight and the measurements are correct, fill a spray bottle with cold water and spray the piece to wet it thoroughly. Leave the piece pinned in place until it is completely dry.

You can also wet the piece before pinning by submerging it in water. Gently squeeze out excess water (do not wring), and then place the piece on your blocking pad and pin it as shown in the illustration below. Allow to the piece to dry completely before unpinning.

Steam blocking involves the use of a steam iron. Position the piece and pin it in place as shown in the illustration. Adjust the iron's heat setting according to the fiber content of the yarn used. Hold the iron several inches above the knit fabric when steaming.

Do not allow the iron to touch the knitted fabric. If you do, you may scorch the yarn or flatten stitches.

SEAMING

We seamed most of the handbags in the book using the mattress stitch, which gives your fabric a clean, seamless look. Instructions for executing the mattress stitch are on page 33.

Wet blocking (left) and steam blocking (right)

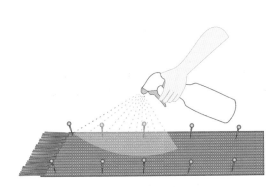
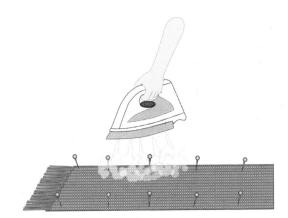

SEWING

Fitting and sewing a lining into your handbag is essential to protect it from stains or sharp objects and to give it a professional look. The lining fabric should be tough yet easy to clean. Don't be afraid to choose a vibrant fabric—although if you are a more traditional type of person, a solid-color lining that matches your knitted bag will certainly do fine. Linings can be hand sewn (using a straight stitch) or sewn on a sewing machine, which is easier and usually produces a better-looking result. The finishing and assembly instructions for each purse in this book give specific details for cutting and sewing the lining for that particular project. Here, however, are some general terms that you should be familiar with before attempting to add the lining to your handbag.

SEAM ALLOWANCE

The seam allowance is an extra amount of fabric added to the actual dimensions of the pattern. It creates a larger border, allowing you to sew the pieces together more easily.

STAY STITCHING

Stay stitching is an extra line of stitches reinforcing a seam to prevent stretching and fraying. It is typically done by machine.

CUTTING A LINING

When adding a lining to a bag, first measure the dimensions of the knitted pieces, then add 1/4" (6mm) seam allowance to every side of each knitted piece, unless the pattern directions instruct otherwise. Cut and stitch around the sides of the lining, keeping the mouth open for inserting into the bag. Attach it to the inside of the bag by whipstitching (see page 34).

INSERTING A ZIPPER

1. Choose a zipper at least 2" (5.1cm) larger than the opening of the bag. Place the zipper inside the bag with right side facing out. With a sharp needle and matching thread, whipstitch the zipper to the inside of the bag as shown in step 1 at right.

2. On the front (outside) of the work, backstitch just below the zipper's teeth. Place the lining over the zipper's edge and whipstitch it into place as shown in step 2.

Step 1

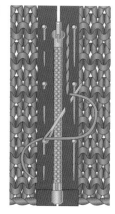

Step 2

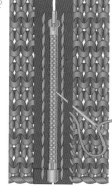

SEWING AND EMBROIDERY STITCHES

MATTRESS STITCH

Knit side (shown): Place the garment pieces you will be joining side by side on a flat surface with the knit side facing up. Insert the needle behind the horizontal bar of the knit stitch on the right-side edge of one garment piece. Repeat for the left-side edge of the other garment piece. Continue joining the pieces, stitching left and right edges together.

Purl side: Place the garment pieces to be joined side by side on a flat surface with the purl side facing up. Insert the needle under one horizontal bar of the purl stitch on the right-side edge of one garment piece, then repeat the same for the left-side edge on the other garment piece.

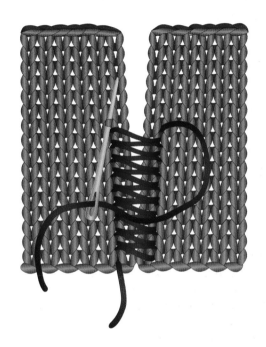

INVISIBLE HORIZONTAL SEAM

With the right sides of the fabric held together so that the stitches are aligned as shown, insert the needle behind one stitch on one piece of the fabric and then behind one stitch on the other piece. Continue as shown.

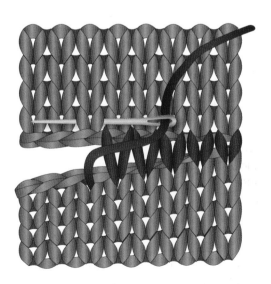

WHIPSTITCH

Thread a tapestry needle with yarn. With either the right or the wrong side of the fabric facing you, insert the tapestry needle through the center of the edge stitches, working from right to left. Start again with the next right-edge stitch, continuing upward until both edges are joined together. Make sure that the stitches are even and do not have gaps when whipping together.

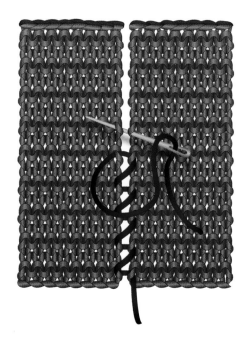

BUTTONHOLE STITCH

Keep the yarn over the edge of the fabric; the beginning of the yarn loop is made. Insert a tapestry needle 1/2"/1.25cm or desired length above the fabric edge. Pull the needle behind the fabric and above the beginning yarn loop. Keep the yarn loop below the needle and pull the needle taut. Repeat this procedure all along the edge of the fabric, keeping the yarn loop below the needle throughout.

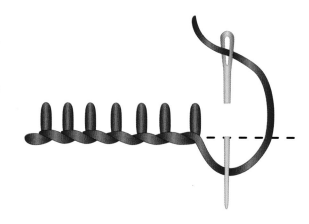

RUNNING STITCH

For this simple and basic embroidery stitch, secure thread with a knot. From the back of the fabric, insert the needle upward through the fabric. Then pass the needle downward through the fabric, spacing stitches evenly.

CHAIN STITCH

Insert the needle through the fabric from back to front. *Form a loop; hold the loop with your thumb. Insert the needle through the original hole from the front of the fabric to the back and bring the needle forward the desired distance. Make sure the needle is inside the loop as you pull the thread through to the front to form the chain. Repeat from *.

LAZY DAISY

Work as for the chain stitch, but anchor the loop at the top of the stitch to form flowers.

FREESTYLE CROSS-STITCH

Secure thread with a knot. Bring the needle through the fabric from the back to the front at Point 1. Pull the thread through. Insert needle at Point 2 and pull thread through to the back. Repeat this motion until the desired number of diagonal lines is formed. Bring the needle to point 7, inserting needle from back to front, and pull thread through. Insert needle at Point 8 to form an X. Repeat this motion until desired number of stitches is formed.

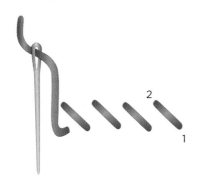
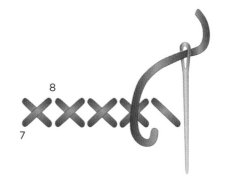

WHIPSTITCH FOR ATTACHMENT OF LINING

Secure the thread with a knot. Beginning at the back of the fabric, insert the needle by catching two layers of fabric, then pull the thread through to the front. Insert the needle from the front to the back of the fabric diagonally, and pull the thread through, making sure that the stitches lie flat.

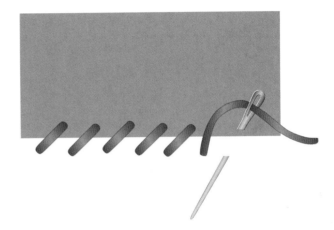

STRINGING BEADS

Cut a small length of thread. Thread a sewing needle, then knot the ends of the thread. Slip the end of the yarn through the loop of thread. Slip beads from the needle through the strand of thread and onto the yarn strand.

SPRING

SPRING GREEN CLUTCH

Reminiscent of the freshest spring growth, this clutch knits up as fast
as the grass grows in April's rains. Knit of nylon yarn in an easy textured stitch and accented with a shiny frog closure and snap, this classic
clutch is sure to enhance all the bright hues of your spring and summer
wardrobe.

SKILL LEVEL
Easy

FINISHED MEASUREMENTS
Body: 7" X 11 1/2"/18 X 29cm (unsewn)
Finished clutch: 7" X 5"/18 X 12.5cm

YARN
1 ball of Feza Yarn Silk (100% nylon yarn, 1 3/4 oz/50g = approx 82 yd/75m per ball) in #636 green OR approximately 82 yd/75m nylon, bulky-weight yarn in green

MATERIALS
- Size 10.5 U.S. (8mm) needles or size needed to obtain gauge
- 1 BagWorks 5/8" gold snap, #A3117-GLD, OR other 5/8" (1.6cm) snap
- 1 Joyce Trimming 3" X 3/8" white frog closure, #GA-17638, OR other 3" X 3/8" (7.6cm X 1cm) frog closure in white
- 1/4 yd (25cm) lining fabric of your choice
- Sewing needle and thread to match the lining
- Fabric glue
- 1 piece 6 1/2"X 11" (16.5cm X 28cm) of buckram fabric
- Scissors
- Tapestry needle
- Matching thread for frog closure
- Iron

GAUGE
14 sts = 4"/10cm over St st
Always take time to check your gauge.

PATTERN NOTES
- Knit loosely throughout.
- The fabric will be a long rectangle, folded at two places.
- For instructions on cutting out lining, see page 32.

SPECIAL ABBREVIATION
Pskb: Pass slip stitch over knit stitch onto LH needle, knit into back of this slipped stitch, drop st from LH needle.

STITCH PATTERN
Parallel Herringbone Stitch
Row 1 (RS): K1, *sl 1, k1, pskb; rep from * to last st, k1.
Row 2: *P2tog, purl first st of the pair again, slipping both sts off needle; rep from * to end.
Rep Rows 1–2 for Parallel Herringbone Stitch patt.

CLUTCH
CO 36 stitches. Work in Parallel Herringbone Stitch patt until piece measures 11 1/2"/29cm. BO on WS.

FINISHING AND ASSEMBLY
1. Weave in ends.
2. With iron on low setting, press lightly on wrong side.
3. Cut lining according to instructions on page 32.
4. Cut out buckram to size of knitted fabric. Trim 1/4" (6mm) around all edges.
5. Glue buckram to WS of knitted fabric, pressing down firmly.
6. Make one marking for snap ball on right side of lining; make second marking for snap socket on top center of RS of knitted fabric. Attach snaps to fabric and lining.
7. Whipstitch lining to knitted fabric.
8. Fold snap-socket panel 4 1/2"/11.4cm over and seam sides.
9. Fold snap-ball panel over so that snaps join.
10. Attach frog closure to front center of clutch.

DESIGN TIP
This clutch can easily be transformed into a wristlet just by adding a wrist strap.

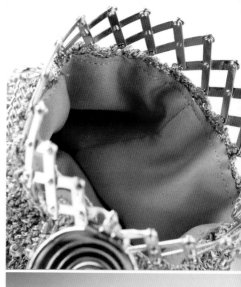

REMINISCENCE COIN PURSE

Reminiscent of bygone days of ball gowns and embroidered silk gloves, this beaded coin purse, in a lovely spring-inspired shade of pink, adds glamour to any outfit. The handy chain lets you wear it as a simple but enchanting evening bag. The puffy lace stitch pattern is both easy and engaging to knit, and the gate purse frame adds an antique touch.

SKILL LEVEL
Easy

FINISHED MEASUREMENTS
Length: 5 1/2"/14cm
Circumference: 10"/25.5cm

YARN
1 ball of Rowan Yarns Lurex Shimmer (80% viscose/20% polyester yarn, 25g = approx 103 yd/95m per ball) in #336 gleam OR approximately 103 yd/95m viscose/polyester blend, fingering-weight yarn in pink

MATERIALS
- Size 5 U.S. (3.75mm) double-pointed needles or size needed to obtain gauge
- Tapestry needle
- Stitch markers
- 1 tube of Blue Moon Beads Czech glass seed bead, #51695, in silver-lined crystal OR 231 11/o seed beads in transparent silver
- 1 Sunbelt Fashion 1 3/16" X 1" gate purse frame, SKU # SF-PF-G01[S], in silver OR other 1 3/16" X 1" (3cm X 2.5cm) gate purse frame in silver
- 1 18" X 1/4"/46cm X 6.4mm round-link chain in silver
- Pliers for attaching chain to gate purse frame
- 1/4 yd (25cm) lining fabric of your choice

GAUGE
26 sts = 4"/10cm over St st
Always take time to check your gauge.

PATTERN NOTES
- The purse is worked from the bottom up on double-pointed needles.
- A chart and written instructions for Puffy Lace Stitch Pattern are provided; choose the instruction method you prefer.
- For instructions on whip-stitching, see page 34.
- For instructions on cutting out lining, see page 32.
- For instructions on stringing beads, see page 37.

SPECIAL ABBREVIATIONS
Inc 1: Increase by knitting into front and back of same stitch.
K2togwb: Knit two stitches together with bead.
Ktbl: Knit through back loop.
K1wb: Knit one stitch with bead.

STITCH PATTERN
**Puffy Lace Stitch
(over a multiple of 10 sts)**
Rnds 1, 2, 3, and 4: Knit.
Rnd 5: *(K5, turn, p5, turn) 3 times, k10; rep from * to end.
Rnds 6, 7, 8, and 9: Knit.
Rnd 10: K5, *(K5, turn, p5, turn) 3 times, k10; rep from * to last 5 sts, (K5, turn, p5, turn) 3 times.
Rnds 11, 12, 13, 14: Knit.

Work rnds 1–14 once for Puffy Lace Stitch patt.

PURSE
String beads onto yarn.
CO 12 stitches. Divide evenly on 3 dpns, pm, and join to begin knitting in the round.
Rnd 1: Knit.
Rnd 2: Purl.
Rnd 3: (Inc 1, k1) across. (18 sts)
Rnd 4: (Inc 1, p2) across. (24 sts)
Rnd 5: Rep rnd 3. (36 sts)
Rnd 6: Rep rnd 4. (48 sts)
Rnd 7: Rep rnd 3. (72 sts)
Rnd 8: Rep rnd 4. (96 sts)
Rnd 9: (Inc 1, k23) across. (100 sts)
Work Puffy Lace Stitch once.
Rnd 24: (K1, k2togwb) across to last 3 sts, k3tog with bead. (66 sts)
Rnd 25: Ktbl across.
Rnd 26: Knit.
Rnd 27: *(K1wb, K1); rep from * across.
Rnd 28: Ktbl across.
Rnd 29: Knit.
Rnd 30: *(K1, k1wb); rep from * across.
Rep rnds 25–30 twice more and rnds 25–27 once more. Knit two rnds. BO all 66 sts.

FINISHING AND ASSEMBLY
1. Weave in ends, being sure to close up the bottom of the knitted pouch.
2. Cut lining according to instructions on page 32.

STITCH CHART
Puffy Lace Stitch
(over a multiple of 10 sts)

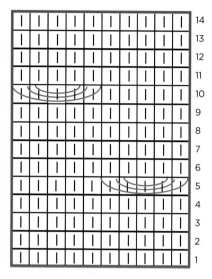

14
13
12
11
10
9
8
7
6
5
4
3
2
1

Work Rounds 1–14 once

Legend

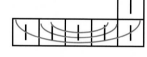

| | Knit |

(K5, turn, p5, turn) 3 times

3. Attach lining to inside of knitted pouch.
4. Expand the gate purse frame and attach by sewing knitted pouch to frame through the holes on the bottom of the purse frame.
5. Open one ring at the end of the silver chain with pliers and attach to side of purse frame. Close the

ring with pliers. Repeat for other end of the chain.

DESIGN TIP
To give this lovely purse a truly unique pattern, use a variety of beads of different colors.

CITRUS SLICE

As vibrant as spring itself, this juicy orange shoulder bag is constructed using short rows. You craft the clever stitch patterns that create the circular shapes of the front and back using only two needles, avoiding the complexity of knitting with four or even five needles. The small *shisha*, or mirror, positioned at the center adds a bit of sparkle to a purse that's sure to put a twinkle in your eye.

SKILL LEVEL

Intermediate

FINISHED MEASUREMENTS

Front and back diameter: 7"/17.8cm

Gusset: 14" X 1 1/2"/35.6cm X 3.8cm

Depth 1 1/2"/3.8cm

YARN

1 skein of Louet Euroflax (100% wet spun linen, 100 grams = approx 190 yd/174m per hank) in #62 Citrus Orange OR approximately 190 yd/174m linen, worsted-weight yarn in bright orange

MATERIALS

- Size 5 U.S. (3.75mm) needles or size needed to obtain gauge
- Cable needle
- 1 UMX 3/8" X 21.5" gold purse chain, #CH-1055-G, OR other 3/8" x 21.5" (.95cm X 55cm) purse chain in gold
- 2 M&J Trimming 15mm (5/8") gold metal D-Rings, # 32345, OR 2 other 15mm (5/8") gold metal D-rings
- 1 package of Darice 1" Round Mirrors, 10 pcs, Item #1613-42, OR 1 1"/2.5cm round mirror
- Tapestry needle
- 1 9"/23cm zipper in orange
- 1/2 yd (50cm) lining fabric of your choice
- 1/4 yd (23cm) buckram
- Fabric glue
- Sewing needle and cotton thread to match the lining

GAUGE

22 sts = 4"/10cm over St st
Always take time to check your gauge.

PATTERN NOTES

- For instructions on whip-stitching, see page 34.
- For instructions on cutting out lining, see page 32.
- The front and back are joined together by the 6-st Cable Stitch patt gusset, leaving a 7"/18cm opening for the zipper.
- A chart and written instructions for 6-st Cable Stitch patt are provided. Choose the instruction method you prefer.

SPECIAL ABBREVIATIONS

4-st Right Cable: Slip 2 sts to cable needle and hold in back of work, k2, k2 from cable needle.

4-st Left Cable: Slip 2 sts to cable needle and hold in front of work, k2, k2 from cable needle.

Turn: Turn work.

STITCH PATTERNS

360° Cable Stitch

Foundation row: K3, p2, k6, p2, k6, p2, k3. (24 sts)

Row 1 (WS): Knit the k sts, purl the p sts, leaving 2 sts on LH needle. Turn.

Row 2: K1, (p2, k2, 4-st Right Cable) twice, p2, k3.

Row 3: Rep row 2, leaving 4 sts on needle. Turn.

Row 4: P1, (4-st Left Cable, k2, p2) twice, k3.

Row 5: Rep row 2, leaving 6 sts on needle. Turn.

Row 6: K1, 4-st Right Cable, p2, k2, 4-st right cable, p2, k3.

Row 7: Rep row 2, leaving 8 sts on needle. Turn.

Row 8: K3, p2, 4-st Left Cable, k2, p2, k3.

Row 9: Rep row 2, leaving 10 sts on needle. Turn.

Row 10: K1, p2, k2, 4-st Right Cable, p2, k3.

Row 11: Rep row 2, leaving 12 sts on needle. Turn.

Row 12: P1, 4-st Left Cable, k2, p2, k3.

Row 13: Rep row 2, leaving 14 sts on needle. Turn.

Row 14: K1, 4-st Right Cable, p2, k3.

Row 15: Knit the k sts, purl the p sts across all sts.

Row 16: K3, (p2, 4-st Left Cable, k2) twice, p2, k3.

Rep rows 1–16 for 360° Cable Stitch patt.

360° Rib Stitch

Foundation row: (K2, p2) six times. (24 sts)

Row 1 (WS): Knit the k sts, purl the p sts leaving 2 sts on LH needle. Turn.

Row 2 and all RS rows: Knit the k sts, purl the purl sts.

Row 3: Rep row 2, leaving 4 sts on needle. Turn.

Row 5: Rep row 2, leaving 6 sts on needle. Turn.
Row 7: Rep row 2, leaving 8 sts on needle. Turn.
Row 9: Rep row 2, leaving 10 sts on needle. Turn.
Row 11: Rep row 2, leaving 12 sts on needle. Turn.
Row 13: Rep row 2, leaving 14 sts on needle. Turn.
Row 15: Knit the k sts, purl the p sts across all 24 sts.
Row 16: Knit the k sts, purl the p sts.
Rep rows 1–16 for 360° Rib Stitch patt.

**6-st Cable Stitch
(over 10 sts)**
Row 1: P2, k2, 4-st Right Cable, p2.
Row 2: K2, p6, k2.
Row 3: P2, 4-st Left Cable, k2, p2.
Row 4: K2, p6, k2.
Rep rows 1–4 for 6-st Cable Stitch patt.

PURSE
Front Body
CO 24 stitches. Work in 360° Cable Stitch patt until a full circle is formed. BO all 24 sts on WS.

Back Body
CO 24 stitches. Work in 360° Rib Stitch patt until a full circle is formed. BO all 24 sts on WS.

Gusset
CO 10 stitches. Work in 6-st Cable Stitch patt until piece measures 14"/35.6cm. BO all 6 sts.

FINISHING AND ASSEMBLY

1. Seam ends of front body together to form a circle, leaving a small hole in the center. Repeat with back body, closing center hole so that no opening remains.
2. Weave in ends.
3. Block knitted fabric.
4. Cut lining according to instructions on page 32.
5. Cut buckram ¼" (6mm) smaller than knitted fabric.
6. Glue mirror on wrong side of bag front, making sure refection can be seen through hole on right side.
7. Glue buckram to wrong side of knitted fabric.
8. Whipstitch knitted pieces together by attaching body to one side of gusset and then repeating for other side, leaving a 7"/17.8cm opening.
9. Sew zipper into opening.
10. Sew lining pieces together, leaving 7"/17.8cm opening for zipper, and whipstitch lining to inside of knitted purse.
11. Thread tapestry needle with yarn. Attach D-rings on both sides of opening, whipstitching through the straight ends of D-rings.
12. Attach gold chain handles to D-rings.

DESIGN TIP
If your stitches are loose in some places and tight in others, try using a smaller needle, which will help you maintain a balanced pattern.

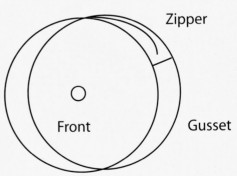

STITCH CHART
6-st Cable Stitch
(over 10 sts)

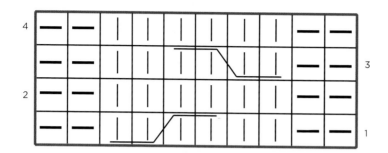

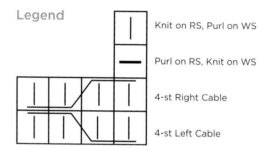

Legend

│	Knit on RS, Purl on WS
—	Purl on RS, Knit on WS
	4-st Right Cable
	4-st Left Cable

STITCH CHART
Fairuz Cable Stitch
(over a multiple of 20 sts)

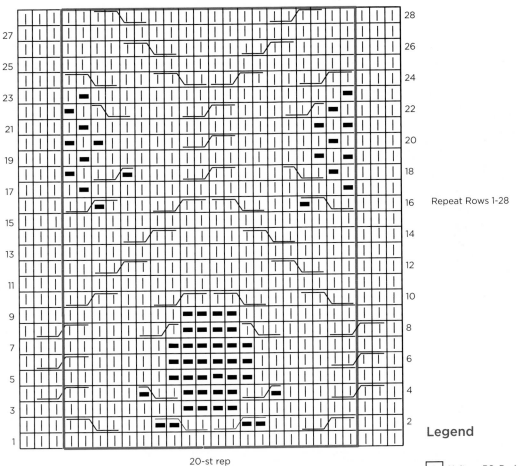

20-st rep

Repeat Rows 1-28

Legend

|	Knit on RS, Purl on WS
▬	Purl on RS, Knit on WS
	3-st Right Purl Cable
	3-st Left Purl Cable
	3-st Right Cable
	3-st Left Cable
	4-st Right Purl Cable
	4-st Left Purl Cable
	4-st Right Cable
	4-st Left Cable
	4-st Left Knit-Purl Twist
	4-st Right Knit-Purl Twist

LAVENDER MESSENGER BAG

Lavender, the ideal springtime neutral, makes this classic tote a great choice for complementing an outfit. The allover twist-stitch pattern creates a rich texture, and the knitted handle adds to the effect. Complete the look by using a vibrant lining fabric and ornate button of your choice.

SKILL LEVEL
Intermediate

FINISHED MEASUREMENTS
Length of body: 9 1/2"/24cm
Width of body: 9 1/2"/24cm
Strap length: 24"/61cm

YARN
1 skein of Coats and Clark Yarn Red Heart Super Saver (100% acrylic yarn, 7 oz/198g = approx 364 yd/333m per skein) in #0579, pale plum, OR approximately 364 yd/333m medium worsted-weight acrylic yarn in pale purple

MATERIALS
- Size 9 U.S. (5.5mm) needles or size needed to obtain gauge
- 1 Joyce Trimming 25mm metal button, #BLU-F4029, in antique nautikes, OR other 25mm shell-shaped metal button
- 1/4 yd (25cm) lining fabric of your choice
- Sewing needle and thread to match the lining
- Measuring tape
- Stitch markers
- Stitch holder
- Tapestry needle

GAUGE
16 sts = 4"/10cm over St st
Always take time to check your gauge.

PATTERN NOTES
- A chart and written instructions for Sandy Twist Stitch patt are provided. Choose the instruction method you prefer.
- For instructions on cutting out lining, see page 32.
- For instructions on whip-stitching, see page 34.

SPECIAL ABBREVIATIONS
LT: With RH needle behind LH needle, skip the first st on LH needle and k second st tbl, insert RH needle into backs of both sts, k2tog tbl.
RT: K2tog, leaving both sts on needle; insert RH needle between 2 sts, and k first st again; sl both sts from needle.
K1tbl: Knit 1 st though the back loop.
Yo2: Yarn over twice.
K2togtbl: K2tog through back loop.

STITCH PATTERNS
Sandy Twist Stitch (over 56 sts)
Row 1 (RS): P5, (RT) 6 times, p4, (RT) 6 times, LT, p4, (LT) 6 times, p5.
Row 2 (WS): K4, p12, k4, p16, k4, p12, k4.
Row 3: P4, (RT) 6 times, p4, (RT) 6 times, (LT) twice, p4, (LT) 6 times, p4.
Row 4: K3, p12, k4, p18, k4, p12, k3.

Row 5: P3, (RT) 6 times, p4, (RT) 6 times, (LT) 3 times, p4, (LT) 6 times, p3.
Row 6: K2, p12, k4, p20, k4, p12, k2.
Row 7: P2, (RT) 6 times, p4, (RT) 6 times, (LT) 4 times, p4, (LT) 6 times, p2.
Row 8: K1, p12, k4, p22, k4, p12, k1.
Row 9: P1, (RT) 6 times, p4, (RT) 6 times, (LT) 5 times, p4, (LT) 6 times, p1.
Row 10: P12, k4, p24, k4, p12.
Row 11: (RT) 6 times, p4, (RT) 6 times, (LT) 6 times, p4, (LT) 6 times.
Row 12: K1, p12, k4, p22, k4, p12, k1.
Row 13: P1, (LT) 6 times, p4, (LT) 5 times, (RT) 6 times, p4, (RT) 6 times, p1.
Row 14: K2, p12, k4, p20, k4, p12, k2.
Row 15: P2, (LT) 6 times, p4, (LT) 4 times, (RT) 6 times, p4, (RT) 6 times, p2.
Row 16: K3, p12, k4, p18, k4, p12, k3.
Row 17: P3, (LT) 6 times, p4, (LT) 3 times, (RT) 6 times, p4, (RT) 6 times, p3.
Row 18: K4, p12, k4, p16, k4, p12, k4.
Row 19: P4, (LT) 6 times, p4, (LT) twice, (RT) 6 times, p4, (RT) 6 times, p4.
Row 20: K5, p12, k4, p14, k4, p12, k5.
Row 21: P5, (LT) 6 times, p4, LT, (RT) 6 times, p4, (RT) 6 times, p5.

Row 22: K6, p12, k4, p12, k4, p12, k6.

Row 23: P6, (LT) 6 times, p4, (RT) 6 times, p4, (RT) 6 times, p6.

Row 24: K5, p12, k4, p14, k4, p12, k5.

Work rows 1–24 once, then rows 1–10 once more for Sandy Twist Stitch patt.

Back Loop Rib Stitch

Row 1 (RS): *K1tbl, p1; rep from * across.

Row 2 (WS): Knit the knit sts, purl the purl sts.

Rep Rows 1–2 for Back Loop Rib Stitch patt.

PURSE

Front and Back (Make 2)

CO 56 stitches. Begin Sandy Twist Stitch Pattern. Work rows 1–24 once, then rows 1–10 once more.

Next row (RS): (P1, k1tbl) 14 times, p2tog, (K1tbl, p1)13 times. (55 sts)

Next row (WS): Knit the knit sts, purl the purl sts.

Next row (RS): K1tbl the knit sts, purl the purl sts.

Rep last two rows for next thirteen rows; end on WS.

Next rows (RS): Work 12 sts in Back Loop Rib Stitch patt, BO 31 sts ribwise, work last 12 stitches in patt. Place first 12 stitches on stitch holder (right strap).

Left Strap

Cont in rib patt, BO 1 st at beg of next three RS rows (9 sts remain). Work in patt as established until handle measures 12"/31cm from top of purse. BO all sts. Repeat for back.

Right Strap

Slip stitches from holder onto LH needle. Rejoin yarn and cont in rib patt, BO 1 st at beg of next three WS rows (9 sts remain). Work in patt as established until strap measures 12"/31cm from top of purse. BO all sts. Repeat for back.

Purse Tab Closure

Pick up 11 stitches from center of back, beginning with a knit stitch. Turn.

Next Row (WS): (P1, k1) across, to last st, p1.

Work in Back Loop Rib Stitch patt for 1 1/2"/3.8cm, end with WS row.

Next row (RS): (K1tbl, p1) twice, k1tbl, yo2, k2togtbl, (p1, k1tbl) twice.

Next row: (P1, k1) twice, p1, k1—dropping extra yo, (p1, k1) twice, p1.

Work in Back Loop Rib Stitch patt until tab measures 3 1/2"/9cm from beg. BO all 11 sts ribwise on WS.

FINISHING AND ASSEMBLY

1. Weave ends in.
2. Cut out lining according to instructions on page 32.
3. For the front, sew ends of right and left straps together, forming one strap. Rep for back.
4. Refer to diagram. With right sides facing, seam sides of knitted pieces along all edges, keeping the top edge of purse unseamed.
5. Seam lining.
6. Place lining inside bag and attach to bag by whipstitching below the straps and along the opening.
7. Center button 1"/2.5cm from top edge of front. Secure button.

DESIGN TIP

Instead of the shell button, try using a magnetic snap closure and accenting the tab with an ornamental button.

Seem sides and handles

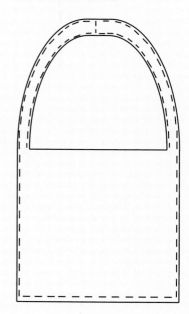

STITCH CHART
Sandy Twist Stitch
(over a multiple of 56 sts)

Work Rows 1-24 once, then
Rows 1-10 once more

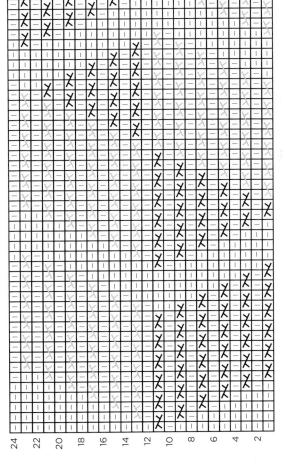

56-st

Legend

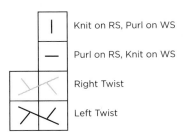

	Knit on RS, Purl on WS
—	Purl on RS, Knit on WS
	Right Twist
	Left Twist

SUMMER

MOOD INDIGO

Nothing says carefree summer living like denim, and this petite indigo shoulder bag will become your summer mainstay for dressing up your casual wear. Just be sure to wash the bag before wearing it, as real indigo dyes tend to run! Super-easy to knit, this purse could be a first cable project.

SKILL LEVEL
Easy

FINISHED MEASUREMENTS
Length: 5"/12.7cm
Height: 8"/20cm

YARN
1 ball of Twilley Denim Freedom (100% cotton yarn, 1 3/4 oz/50g = approx 102 yd/93m per ball), in #102 Denim, OR approximately 102 yd/93m DK-weight cotton yarn in a denim blue color

MATERIALS
- Size 6 U.S. (4.0mm) needles or size needed to obtain gauge
- Cable needle
- Tapestry needle
- Stitch markers
- 1 M&J Trimmings 2 1/2" X 4 1/2 " metal handbag frame, # 28117, in silver, OR other 2 1/2" X 4 1/2" (6 X 11cm) metal handbag frame in silver
- 1/2 yd (50cm) denim fabric at least 45" in width
- 1 package (10 pcs) Tandy Leather Factory's Solid Nickel Plate 3/4" Rings, #1180-10 OR 3 solid nickel plate 3/4" (2cm) rings
- Sewing needle
- Cotton thread to match lining

GAUGE
20.5 sts = 4"/10cm over St st before washing
Always take time to check your gauge.

PATTERN NOTES
- The indigo dye in the yarn will stain your hands slightly when knitting, but it will easily wash off. Make sure your hands are dry when handling the yarn.
- Be sure to wash the knitted pieces before assembly, since the colors will run and the pieces will shrink. The yarn to be used for assembly should be secured by a rubber band and washed with the knitted pieces so that it becomes the same color as the knitted pieces.

SPECIAL ABBREVIATION
4-st Right Cable: Slip 2 sts to cable needle and hold in back of work, k2, k2 from cable needle.

STITCH PATTERNS
4-st Cable Stitch
Row 1 (WS): K2, p4, k2.
Row 2 (RS): P2, k4, p2.
Row 3: K2, p4, k2.
Row 4: P2, 4-st Right Cable, p2.
Rep rows 1–4 for 4-st Cable Stitch patt.

Rib Stitch
Row 1 (RS): *K1, p1; rep from * to end.
Row 2 (WS): K the knit sts, p the purl sts.
Rep Row 2 for Rib Stitch patt.

PURSE
Front and Back (Make 2)
CO 40 stitches. Knit two rows. Work in St st for 1 1/2"/4cm, ending on RS. Cont in St st, dec 1 st at the beg and end of every WS row 3 times (34 sts). Work even in patt until piece measures 3"/8cm from cast-on edge. Con in St st, dec 1 st at the beg and end of every WS row 7 times (20 sts). Knit next row. BO all sts on WS.

Cable Trim (Make 2)
CO 8 sts. Complete 4-st Cable Stitch patt 5 times, ending with row 2 (22 rows). BO all sts on WS.

Cable Pocket
CO 20 sts.
Work in Rib Stitch patt for 4 rows.
Row 5 (RS): K6, p2, k4, p2, k6.
Row 6: P6, k2, p4, k2, p6.
Row 7: K6, p2, 4-st Right Cable, p2, k6.
Row 8: P6, k2, p4, k2, p6.
Work rows 5–8 until pocket measures 3 1/2"/9cm from cast-on edge. BO all sts.

WASHING
Wrap remaining yarn and secure with a rubber band.

Wash all pieces according to directions. Allow to air dry completely.

FINISHING AND ASSEMBLY
Attaching Cable Trim to Front
Refer to photo. Slip 1"/2.5cm end of cable trim over ring and sew into place. Slip 1"/2.5cm end of second cable trim over ring and sew into place. Place unsewn end of cable trim on top of front and sew into place. Place unsewn end of second cable trim on bottom of front and sew into place.

Attaching Cable Pocket to Back
Refer to photo below. Place cable pocket at center bottom of back. Sew in place along the sides and bottom of pocket.

Assembling Purse
1. Weave in ends.
2. Block knitted fabric.
3. Cut lining according to instructions on page 32.
4. Whipstitch sides of knitted fabric.
5. Attach silver frame to knitted fabric through attachment holes using sewing thread.
6. Position silver ring below side edge of frame. Whipstitch bottom half of ring, leaving top half unsewn. Repeat for other side.
7. Sew sides of lining and attach to inside of bag.
8. Cut 40" X 2"/101cm X 5cm denim strip. Fold lengthwise and stitch into place. Finished strap should measure approx. 40" X 1"/101cm X 2.5cm.
9. Whipstitch denim strip to side silver ring. Repeat for other side.

DESIGN TIP
If you prefer an adjustable strap, just add a buckle.

ICE CUBE

What has a compact geometric shape, an icy color, and is refreshing to wear on a hot summer day? An ice cube of a bag, of course! The Puff Stitch is easy to knit, and the bag is the perfect size for daily use. The garter-stitch side supports, D-ring closure, and chrome rivets add just the right touch of industrial chic to complete the look.

SKILL LEVEL
Easy

FINISHED MEASUREMENTS
Height: 8 1/2"/22cm from base to bottom of ring handle
Width: 8 1/2"/22cm
Depth: 2"/5cm

YARN
1 skein of Patons Katrina (92% rayon/8% polyester yarn, 3 1/2 oz/100g = approx 163 yd/150m per skein) in #10217 frost OR approximately 163 yd/150m medium-weight rayon/polyester blend yarn in ice blue

MATERIALS
- Size 9 U.S. (5.5mm) needles or size needed to obtain gauge
- Tapestry needle
- Stitch markers
- 1/4 yd (25cm) fusible felt
- 1/4 yd (25cm) lining fabric of your choice
- Sewing needle and cotton thread to match the lining
- 2 M&J Trimming 5.75" metallic acrylic ring handles in silver, #27365, OR a pair of 5.75" (14.6cm) silver metallic acrylic ring handles
- 1 package (96 pcs) M&J Trimming's Ss40 Dome Nailheads 4-Prong in silver, #04040-S, OR 16 silver Ss40 4-prong dome nailheads
- 1 BagWorks Additions 1" (2.5cm) Swivel snap hook

in silver, #A3124-SIL OR one 1" (2.5cm) silver swivel snap hook
- 1 package (4 pcs) Dritz Bag Boutique 1" (2.5cm) D-rings in silver, # 9830, OR one 1" (2.5cm) silver D-ring in silver
- 1 package (4 pcs) BagWorks Silver Foot Brads, #A3116-SIL, OR 2 pairs of 1/2" (12mm) silver purse feet
- 1 piece Tandy Leather Factory Deertan Cowhide Trim, 9 1/4" X 3 3/8", #4036-33 OR one 9 1/4" X 3 3/8" (23.5 X 9cm) gold deertan cowhide trim
- Scissors
- Sewing machine to attach leather to purse (optional) OR leather sewing needle and cotton sewing thread
- 2 sheets of plastic canvas, 7-mesh per inch

GAUGE
18 sts = 4"/10cm over St st
Always take time to check your gauge.

PATTERN NOTES
- Place markers between the increase sts at each end and the pattern in the middle. Knit the inc sts on RS rows; purl these sts on the WS. When you have increased five sts at each end of a row, remove the marker, increase into first and last sts in the row, and incorporate the other four sts into the pattern, adding one pattern

repeat on each side of the piece.
- A chart and written instructions for Puff Stitch patt are provided. Choose the instruction method you prefer.
- For instructions on whipstiching, see page 34.
- For instructions on cutting out lining, see page 32.

SPECIAL ABBREVIATIONS
P3tog: Purl 3 stitches together.
Inc 1: Knit into front, then into back of stitch.
M1: Insert LH needle from front to back into the horizontal strand between the last stitch worked and the next stitch on LH needle. Pick up this strand and knit through the back loop.

STITCH PATTERN
Puff Stitch
(over a multiple of 4 sts)
Row 1 (WS): *(K1, yo, k1) into next st, p3tog; rep from * to end.
Row 2: *P1, k3; rep from * to end.
Row 3: *P3tog, (K1, yo, k1) into next st; rep from * to end.
Row 4: *K3, p1; rep from * to end.
Rep rows 1–4 for Puff Stitch patt.

PURSE
Body (Make 2)
CO 28 stitches. Beg Puff Stitch patt. At the same time, inc 1 st

at the beg and M1 at the end of every row until there are 52 sts on needle. Work every group of four inc sts at each end into patt as described in Pattern Notes, opposite. Work Puff Stitch patt over 52 sts until piece measures 8 1/2"/22cm from beg. End on WS. Bind off 1 st at beg and end of every row until 30 sts remain. BO all sts on WS.

Side Supports (Make 2)

CO 8 sts. Work in garter stitch until 15 ridges are formed. BO all sts.

Strip Closure

CO 6 stitches. Work in garter stitch until 29 ridges are formed. BO all sts.

D-Ring Holder

CO 6 stitches. Work in garter stitch until 6 ridges are formed. BO all sts.

FINISHING AND ASSEMBLY

1. Weave in ends.
2. Block knitted pieces.
3. Cut fusible felt 1/4" (6mm) smaller than the bodies and the side supports. Glue to wrong side of bodies and side supports; press down firmly. Set aside.
4. Cut two pieces of plastic canvas 1/4" (6mm) smaller than the bodies. Set aside.
5. Cut two 5" X 2"/12.7cm X 5cm leather pieces for the

side panels. Cut one 8 1/2" X 2"/22cm X 5cm leather piece for the base panel.

6. Seam base panel to side panels, joining at 2"/5.1cm sides. Hem top of both side panels.
7. Cut lining with 1/4" (6mm) seam allowance for body, base, and side panels. Sew lining pieces together, keeping top edge unsewn.
8. With sewing machine (using straight stitch) or threaded leather needle (using whipstitch), attach leather piece to sides of knitted bodies on wrong side of bag. Refer to photo on following page for details.
9. Mark places for feet at the two corners of the base and attach feet.
10. Whipstitch plastic canvas to wrong side of bodies.
11. Carefully turn bag inside out so that right side of bag is facing outside.
12. Fold top edge of bag over silver handle and whipstitch in place. (See photo on following page.) Repeat for other side.
13. Insert lining and whipstitch top edge of lining just below handles and along the open side ends.
14. Place side support over seamed area of leather panel, hiding leather seams.
15. Position and attach nail heads on four corners of

front and back of side support (eight nail heads on each side support). Repeat for other side.

16. Whipstitch side supports into place.
17. Whipstitch D-ring holder to straight side of D-ring. Attach holder 2 1/2"/6.4cm above bottom of front body.
18. Attach strip closure to swivel hook and position strip closure in center of back body, 4 1/2"/11.5cm above bottom. Secure using whipstitch. Whipstitch up to the top edge of back body.
19. Pull strip closure through handles and in front of bag; hook into D-ring.

DESIGN TIP

If you prefer not to use plastic canvas, you can stabilize your bag using cardboard sandwiched between pieces of adhesive felt.

STITCH CHART
Puff Stitch
(over a multiple of 4 sts)

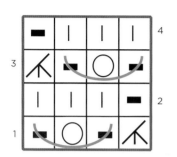

Repeat Rows 1–4

Legend

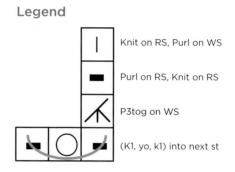

$\vert$	Knit on RS, Purl on WS
▬	Purl on RS, Knit on RS
人	P3tog on WS
◡	(K1, yo, k1) into next st

SUNSHINE HOBO

With its sunshiny yellow color, wooden beads, and rattan handle, this bag shouts summer fun! Knit in a simple textured knit-purl stitch, this hobo works up quickly and easily. It's large and sturdy enough to carry everything you need for a day in the sun—including your latest *One Ball Knits* project.

SKILL LEVEL

Easy

FINISHED MEASUREMENTS

Length: 5"/12.7cm
Width: 13 1/2"/34.3cm

YARN

1 hank of Louet Euroflax (100% wet spun linen yarn, 100g = approx 190 yd/174m per hank) in #05, Goldilocks, OR approximately 190 yd/174m medium-weight wet spun linen yarn in curry yellow

MATERIALS

- Size 10 U.S. (6mm) needles or size needed to obtain gauge
- 2 Sunbelt Fashion Rattan Purse Handles, 7 1/16" (18cm), SKU: SFPH-R15[CO], in Coffee, OR pair of 7 1/16" (18cm) coffee-colored rattan purse handles
- 2 1"/25mm (10mm hole) wooden beads in natural
- 3 1"/25mm (10mm hole) wooden beads in brown
- 1/4 yd (25cm) lining fabric of your choice
- Sewing needle and thread to match the lining
- Stitch markers
- Tapestry needle
- Measuring tape

GAUGE

14 sts = 4"/10cm over St st using double strand of yarn Always take time to check your gauge.

PATTERN NOTES

- Two strands of yarn are used throughout the pattern, except when attaching the handle to the purse.
- The first and last twelve stitches are worked in Texture Stitch. The center stitches are worked in Stockinette Stitch.
- The number of stitches is increased after the first marker and before the second marker, for a total of 2 increased stitches.
- Be sure to notice the difference between the two kinds of increases (Inc 1 and M1) in the instructions.
- For instructions on working 3-needle bind off, see page 27.
- For instructions on cutting out lining, see page 32.

SPECIAL ABBREVIATIONS

Pm: Place marker
Sm: Slip marker
Inc 1: Knit into front, then into back of stitch.
P2tog: Purl two stitches together.
K2tog: Knit two stitches together.
M1: Insert LH needle from front to back into the horizontal strand between the last stitch worked and the next stitch on LH needle. Pick up this strand and knit through the back loop.
St st: Knit RS rows, purl WS rows

STITCH PATTERN

Texture Stitch
Rows 1 and 3 (RS): Knit
Row 2 (WS): *(P2tog, k2tog) in the next two sts, drop both sts from LH needle; rep from * across.
Row 4: P1, rep from * of Row 2 to last st, p1.
Rep rows 1–4 for Texture Stitch patt.

PURSE

Front and Back Body (Make 2)
Unwind half the ball, cut yarn at midpoint.
Prep Rows: Holding two strands of yarn together, CO 36 sts. Work Prep rows 1 and 2 once.
Prep row 1: K12, pm, k12, pm, k12.
Prep row 2: K12, sm, p12, sm, k12.
Row 1 (RS): Work row 1 of Texture Stitch patt over 12 sts, sm, inc 1, k11, m1, sm, work row 1 of Texture Stitch patt over 12 sts. Continue to work first and last 12 sts in texture patt, keeping sts between markers in St st. At the same time, increase 1 st after the first stitch marker and before the second stitch

marker on every RS until there are 48 sts (24 sts St st in the center). Increase 2 sts in the center on every sixth row once more (50 sts). Work four rows even. End on WS. Place stitches on stitch holder, cable needle, or extra needle.

JOINING FRONT AND BACK BODY

Join bottom seam using 3-needle bind off (see page 27).

FINISHING AND ASSEMBLY

1. Weave in ends.
2. Block knitted fabric.
3. Cut out lining according to instructions on page 32.

4. With right sides facing, seam sides of knitted pieces, leaving 2"/5cm unsewn on both top side edges. Turn bag right side out.
5. Place rattan handles over top edge of knitted piece.
6. With one strand of yarn and tapestry needle, whip-stitch handles to body of bag.
7. Sew side seams of lining as for bag, leaving 2"/5cm from top unsewn on side edges.
8. Place lining inside bag and attach to bag by whip-stitching at side edges and below the handles.
9. Place beads on one side of bag (refer to photo below),

and secure in place with tapestry needle and thread.

DESIGN TIP

You can use a curved tapestry needle to attach the rattan handles to the body of the bag.

ORCHID DRAWSTRING POUCH

Plenty of room to carry everything you need, wrapped up in a lovely goes-with-everything summer color—that's what you get when you make this drawstring pouch. The smocking stitch gives a show-off look with very little effort. The entire bag is knit in the round, so no shaping is necessary.

SKILL LEVEL
Intermediate

FINISHED MEASUREMENTS
Height: 6 1/2"/16cm
Circumference at top edge: 22"/56cm

YARN
1 skein Brown Sheep Lamb's Pride Worsted (85% wool/15% mohair, 113g = approx 190 yd/174m) in #M102 Orchid Twist OR approximately 190 yd/174m worsted-weight wool/mohair yarn in orchid

MATERIALS
- Size 8 U.S. (5mm) double-pointed and circular needles or size needed to obtain gauge
- 1 package (10 pcs) of Prym-Dritz Prym Sewing 7/16"/1.1cm Extra-Large Eyelets OR eight 7/16"/1.1cm eyelets
- 1 set of Dritz Bag Boutique Magnetic Snaps (3/4"/1.9cm) in silver #9840 OR 1 set of 3/4"/1.9cm silver magnetic snaps
- Stitch marker
- Tapestry needle
- 1/2 yard (50cm) fusible fleece
- 1/2 yd (50cm) lining fabric of your choice
- Sewing needle and thread to match the lining
- Measuring tape
- Iron

GAUGE
18 sts = 4"/10cm over St st
Always take time to check your gauge.

PATTERN NOTES
- The bag is knit in the round from the base up. Begin with double-pointed needles, changing to circular needle when bag becomes larger.
- For stability, the double-layer lining encloses a layer of fusible fleece.
- For instructions on making I-cord, see page 26.
- For instructions on cutting out lining, see page 32.
- For instructions on whip-stitching, see page 34.

SPECIAL ABBREVIATIONS
Dpn: double-pointed needle
Inc 1: Increase by knitting into front, then into the back of the same stitch
P2tog: Purl two stitches together.
Rnd: Round.
Smocking Loop st: With yarn in back, insert RH needle between the 6th and 7th sts on the LH needle. Wrap yarn around the RH needle and draw it forward, forming a loop. Slip this loop onto the LH needle, and knit it together with the first st on the LH needle.

STITCH PATTERN
Smocking Stitch
Rnds 1, 2, and 3: *P2, k2; rep from * to end.
Rnd 4: P2, *Smocking Loop st, k1, p2, k2, p2; rep from * to last 4 sts, p2, k2.
Rnds 5, 6, and 7: Rep rnd 1.
Rnd 8: P2, k2, p2, *Smocking Loop st, k1, p2, k2, p2; rep from * to last 2 sts. Remove stitch marker, work Smocking Loop st, k1. Replace stitch marker in the original position. Rep rnds 1–8 for Smocking Stitch patt.

PURSE
Base
CO 12 stitches. Divide evenly on three dpns, pm to mark beg of rnd.
Rnd 1 (WS): Knit.
Rnd 2 and all even rnds: Purl.
Rnd 3: (Inc 1, k1) across. (18 sts)
Rnd 5: (Inc 1, k2) across. (24 sts)
Rnd 7: (Inc 1, k3) across. (30 sts)
Rnd 9: (Inc 1, k4) across. (36 sts)
Rnd 11: (Inc 1, k5) across. (42 sts)
Rnd 13: (Inc 1, k6) across. (48 sts)
Rnd 15: (Inc 1, k7) across. (54 sts)
Rnd 17: (Inc 1, k8) across. (60 sts)
Rnd 19: (Inc 1, k9) across. (66 sts)

Rnd 21: (Inc 1, k10) across. (72 sts)

Rnd 23: (Inc 1, k5) across. (84 sts)

Rnd 25: (Inc 1, k6) across. (96 sts)

Rnd 27: (Inc 1, k7) across. (108 sts)

Purl one round.

Next round: Switch to circular needle and (p2tog, p25) 4 times. (104 sts)

Body

Begin Smocking Stitch patt. Work rows 1–8 three times. Rep rnd 1 seven times.

Hem

(Knit 1 round, purl 1 round) four times. BO all 104 sts.

I-Cord Handle

CO 4 sts, work I-cord until cord measures 45"–50"/114–127cm. BO all 4 sts.

FINISHING AND ASSEMBLY

1. Weave in ends.
2. Add eyelets to top edge of bag, according to manufacturer's directions. You may need to use your fingers to make a hole large enough to fit the eyelet.
3. Cut 2 sets of base and body linings according to instructions on page 32. Cut one set of fusible fleece lining.
4. Iron fusible fleece onto one side of body and base lining.
5. Sew body of lining to base of lining. Repeat for second lining (2 linings are made).
6. Attach both linings with right sides together, keeping 4"/10cm on top edge unstitched. Using the 4"/10cm opening, pull right side of linings through and shape so that one body

and base lining is inside the other. Whipstitch the 4"/10cm opening.
7. Mark placement of magnetic snaps and attach snaps to bag.
8. Place the lining inside the bag, covering the wrong side of the eyelets. Whipstitch lining to top edge of bag.
9. Stay stitch 2"/5cm below edge of bag, through lining and bag, making sure you are well below the eyelets. The stay stitching will keep the I-cord in place.
10. Weave I-cord through the eyelets and seam ends together.

DESIGN TIP

If fusible felt interfacing is not available, then adhesive felt or lightweight batting will do.

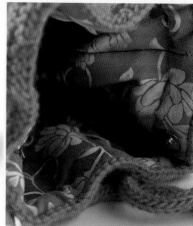

SUMMER BRIGHT

Colors evoking the heat of summer shimmer across this mohair hand-bag. Neither too small nor too large, this bag is a very convenient size for daily necessities. The bright colors come from a multihued yarn felted and embellished with straight-stitch embroidery. Knitting couldn't be easier, as no shaping is required—you just knit two stockinette-stitch pieces and felt them. The hardware gives this bag an added flare.

STITCH GUIDE

SCHEMATIC GUIDE

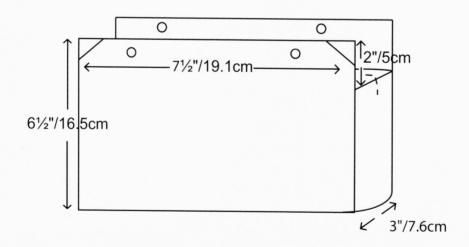

7½"/19.1cm

2"/5cm

6½"/16.5cm

3"/7.6cm

FALL

BLACK PEARL

Be ready for glamorous autumn nights with this elegant evening bag. The star stitch looks intricate but works up easily, and the entire bag will be completed quickly, using up your entire hank of yarn. The pearl handle adds an elegant touch and helps to warm those chilly but festive evenings.

SKILL LEVEL
Easy

FINISHED MEASUREMENTS
Length: 4 1/2"/11.4cm
Width: 4 1/2"/11.4cm
Depth: 4"/10.2cm

YARN
1 hank of Berroco Bonsai (97% bamboo/3% nylon, 1.75 oz/50g = approx 77 yd/71m per hank) in #4134 Sumi Ink OR approximately 77 yd/71m medium-weight bamboo/nylon blend yarn in black

MATERIALS
- Size 8 U.S. (5mm) needles or size needed to obtain gauge
- Tapestry needle
- 1 Sunbelt Fashion Classic/Vintage Purse Frame, 2 7/8" X 6", SKU: SFPH-15 in silver OR other 2 7/8" (7.3cm) X 6" (15.2cm) vintage silver purse frame
- 1 Sunbelt Fashion Plastic Beaded Purse Handle, 13 1/2" (34cm) loose wire, SKU: SFPH-BP04 OR other 13 1/2" (34cm) plastic beaded purse handle
- 1 package (4 pcs) BagWorks Additions Silver Foot Brad, #A3116-SIL, in silver OR four 1/2" (12mm) silver purse feet
- 1 package (4 pcs) BagWorks Additions Silver Crimp, #A3115-SIL, OR two 1/2" (12mm) silver crimps
- 1 package Dritz Innerfuse

Double-Sided Stiff Fusible Interfacing, 14" X 18", Heavyweight #8306 OR other 14" X 18" (35.56cm X 45.72cm) heavyweight double-sided stiff fusible interfacing
- 18 6mm white pearl beads
- 1 spool of invisible thread, 1 spool of black thread, and sewing needle
- Fabric glue
- 1/4 yd (23cm) lightweight lining fabric of your choice
- 1/4 yd (23cm) lightweight interfacing
- Pliers (optional)

GAUGE
18 sts = 4"/10cm over St st
Always take time to check your gauge.

PATTERN NOTES
- The base and one side of the bag will be knitted first as a single piece. The other three sides will be picked up and knitted from the base.
- A chart and written instructions for Star Stitch pattern are provided. Choose the instruction method you prefer.
- Beads are attached later, after knitting and seaming sides of bags.
- Knitting this purse uses the entire ball of yarn. Use invisible thread to attach the beads and seam the purse.
- For instructions on cutting out lining, see page 32.
- For instructions on whipstiching, see page 34.

SPECIAL ABBREVIATION
5-Star: (P5tog leaving sts on LH needle, yo) twice, p5tog dropping worked stitches off LH needle.

PATTERN STITCH
Star Stitch (over 21 sts)
Row 1 and every RS row: Knit.
Row 2: Purl.
Row 4: P3, make 5-Star, p5, make 5-star, p3.
Row 6: Purl.
Row 8: P8, make 5-star, p8.
Rep rows 2–8 once, 1–8 twice, and rows 1–3 once for Star Stitch patt.

PURSE
Base and One Side
CO 17 sts. Work in Garter St for 21 ridges end on RS. (The base is made.)
Next row (WS): Purl.
Next rows (RS): Knit.
Work in St st for 27 rows. BO all 17 sts. (One side is made.)

Second Side
Pick up and k 17 sts along the CO edge. Work in St st for 27 rows. BO all 17 sts. (The second side is made.)

Front
Pick up and k 21 sts along the garter st portion of one long side. Work Star Stitch patt: work rows 2–8 once, work rows 1–8 twice, and work rows 1–3 once. BO all 21 sts.

Back

Pick up and k 21 sts along the garter st portion of the opposite side. Work Star Stitch patt: work rows 2–8 once, work rows 1–8 twice, and work rows 1–3 once. BO all 21 sts.

FINISHING AND ASSEMBLY

1. Attach beads below each 5-star stitch.
2. Weave in ends.
3. Block knitted fabric.
4. Cut out lining according to instructions on page 32.
5. Cut lightweight interfacing the same size as knitted piece, then trim 1/4" (6mm) on all sides.

6. Cut heavyweight double-sided stiff fusible interfacing to same size as base of knitted piece.
7. Glue heavyweight double-sided stiff fusible interfacing to wrong side of base. Set aside to dry.
8. Mark position of purse feet and attach four feet to the bottom of purse.
9. Glue lightweight interfacing to wrong side of knitted fabric, including the base, to cover heavyweight interfacing. Set aside to dry.
10. Seam sides of knitted pieces together with invisible thread.
11. Attach knitted pieces to purse frame using black thread.

12. Sew fabric lining.
13. Hem top edge of lining, turning 1/4" (6mm) under and sewing by hand or machine.
14. Carefully glue top edge of lining to the inside of frame above the knitted fabric. Allow to dry completely.
15. Slip wire loop of beaded handle through purse frame hole. Secure with invisible thread.
16. Place crimp over wire loop and clamp together.
17. Repeat steps 15 and 16 for other side.

DESIGN TIP

This purse would make a lovely bridal accessory—just change the color to match the gown.

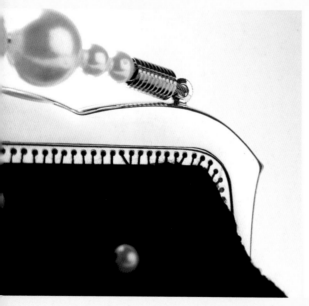

STITCH CHART
Star Stitch
(over 21 sts)

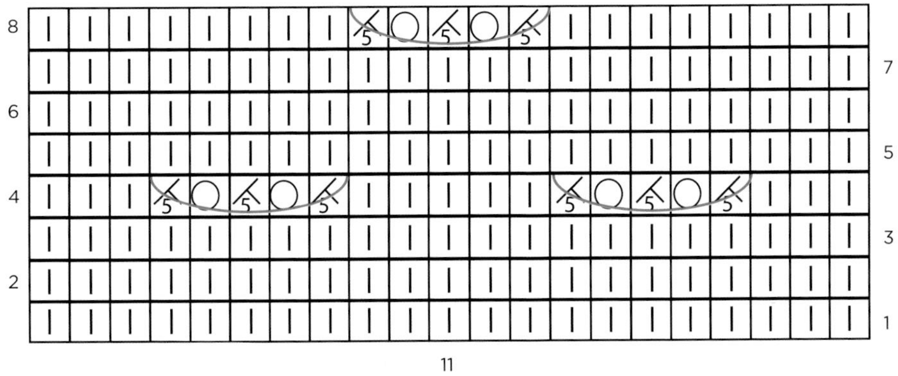

Work Rows 2-8 once,
rows 1-8 twice, and
rows 1-3 once

Legend

I	Knit on RS, Purl on WS
5-Star chart symbols	5-Star

HARVEST MOON

Imagine a huge, golden harvest moon risen just halfway over the horizon. That's the effect of this handy-sized felted tote, ornamented with gold-embellished black handles and round golden studs. This project uses pleats, formed by shaping the felted fabric as it dries, to create an interesting textural effect. The zippered closure finishes off this substantial bag neatly and completely.

SKILL LEVEL
Intermediate

FINISHED MEASUREMENTS
Height: 6"/15cm
Width: 12"/30cm
Depth: 1"/2.5cm

YARN
1 hank of Berroco Ultra Alpaca (50% alpaca/50% wool, 3.5 oz/100g = approx 215 yd/198m per hank) in color #6229, sweet potato, OR approximately 215 yd/197m medium weight alpaca/wool blend yarn in golden brown

MATERIALS
- Size 8 U.S. (5mm) double-pointed and circular needles or size needed to obtain gauge
- 1 BagWorks Additions 5 1/2" Gold Purse Handle, #A2603-GLD, OR other 5" (12.7cm) purse handle in gold
- 1 package (4 pcs) BagWorks Additions Gold Foot Brads, #A3116-GLD, OR two 1/2" (12mm) gold purse feet from another maker
- 1 package (96 pcs) M&J Trimming Ss40 Dome Nailheads, 4-Prong, Gold, #04040-G OR 24 4-prong dome nailheads in gold
- Straight pins
- Stitch markers
- Tapestry needle
- 1 10" (25.5cm) zipper in chocolate brown
- 1/4 yd (23cm) lining fabric of your choice
- 1 sheet of plastic canvas
- Sewing needle and thread to match the lining.

GAUGE
20 sts and 26 rows = 4"/10cm over St st before felting
Always take time to check your gauge.

PATTERN NOTES
- For instructions on whip-stiching, see page 34.
- For instructions on cutting out lining, see page 32.
- Place markers between the increase sts at each end and the pattern in the middle.
- For instructions on felting, see page 30.

SPECIAL ABBREVIATIONS
N1: Needle 1.
N2: Needle 2.
N3: Needle 3.
Rnd: Round.
Inc 1: Knit into front, then into back of stitch.

STITCH PATTERN
Stringy Lace Stitch (over an odd number of stitches)
Row 1: *K2, (yo, pull the last st on RH needle over the yo) 5 times; rep from *, end k1.
Row 2: K1, rep from * of row 1 across to last 2 sts, end k2.
Rep rows 1–2 twice for Stringy Lace Stitch patt.

PURSE
CO 9 st. Divide evenly on three dpns and pm to mark beg of rnd.
Rnd 1: Knit.
Rnd 2 and all WS rows: Purl.
Rnd 3: (K1, inc 1) across to last st, k1. (13 sts)
    N1: 4 sts
    N2: 5 sts
    N3: 4 sts
Rnd 5: (K1, inc 1) across to last st, k1 (19 sts)
    N1: 6 sts
    N2: 7 sts
    N3: 6 sts
Rnd 7: (K1, inc 1) across to last st, k1 (28 sts)
    N1: 9 sts
    N2: 10 sts
    N3: 9 sts
Rnd 9: (K1, inc 1) across to two sts, k1, inc 1 (42 sts)
    N1: 13 sts
    N2: 15 sts
    N3: 14 sts
Rnd 11: (K1, inc 1) across to two sts, k1, inc 1 (63 sts)
    N1: 19 sts
    N2: 23 sts
    N3: 21 sts
Rnd 13: (K1, inc 1) across to last st, k1 (94 sts)
    N1: 28 sts
    N2: 35 sts
    N3: 31 sts
Rnd 15: (K1, inc 1) across to two sts, k1, inc 1 (141 sts)
    N1: 42 sts
    N2: 52 sts
    N3: 47 sts
Rnd 17: Change to circular needle, (K1, inc 1) around to

last st, k1. (211 sts)
(P 1 rnd, k 1 rnd) 4 times. Purl next 3 rnds. Bind off.

FELTING

For general instructions on felting, see page 30. It generally takes 10 to 15 minutes to felt the fabric. Check fabric frequently during felting and stop the process when fabric has shrunk to desired size. The outer edge will be looser than the rest of the fabric. The felted fabric should have a diameter of 7 1/2"/19cm.

DRYING THE FABRIC

Lay fabric on flat surface. Form 10 pleats spaced 1 1/2–2"/3.8–5cm apart, poking straight pins through fabric to secure the pleats. Dry with pleats in place.

STRINGY LACE STITCH BORDER

Pick up and k 185 sts around perimeter of fabric. When picking up sts, poke needle in 1/8" (.32cm) from edge of fabric. For pleats, poke needle through all layers of fabric to secure pleat. Work 4 rnds in Stringy Lace Stitch patt. BO all sts.

EDGING AND BASE

CO 9 stitches. Work in garter st until strip measures 42"/107cm (57 ridges). Felt strip for purse edging. Allow to dry completely.

FINISHING AND ASSEMBLY

1. Weave in ends.
2. Block knitted pieces.
3. Whipstitch felted strip around outer edge of lace pattern.
4. Cut off remaining part of felted strip. Fold bag in half so that it forms a half-moon shape.
5. Cut a strip approx 9 1/2" X 1"/24.13cm X 2.54cm from the remaining felted strip.
6. Cut a strip approx 9 1/2" X 1"/24.13cm X 2.54cm of plastic canvas.
7. Cut out lining with 1/4" (6mm) seam allowance for body.
8. Position plastic canvas over base, trimming canvas to fit without overlapping. Whipstitch plastic canvas to base.
9. Attach base strip to outside of bag by whipstitching in center of fold using same yarn.
10. Mark places for feet and attach feet to both ends of base.
11. Mark places for nine nail heads at equal intervals around top edge of bag

and three nail heads under pleated felt near base. Refer to photo and diagram opposite for placement. Repeat for other side.

12. Position purse handles above lace pattern and attach to felted strip according to manufacturer's directions. Repeat for other side.
13. Fold knitted bag over and whipstitch side seams, beginning at fold and ending approx 2"/5cm up from each edge as shown in diagram.
14. Fold lining over and sew side seams as for bag.
15. Position zipper inside center of bag and whipstitch into place.
16. Position lining inside bag. Fold lining edge to inside and whipstitch to felted strip below zipper edge.

DESIGN TIP

For an even more glamorous look, use rhinestones instead of gold nailheads.

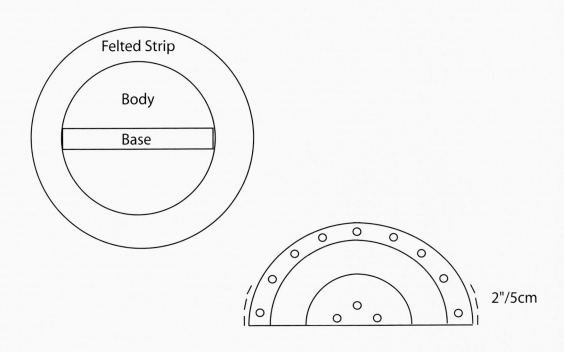

Felted Strip

Body

Base

2"/5cm

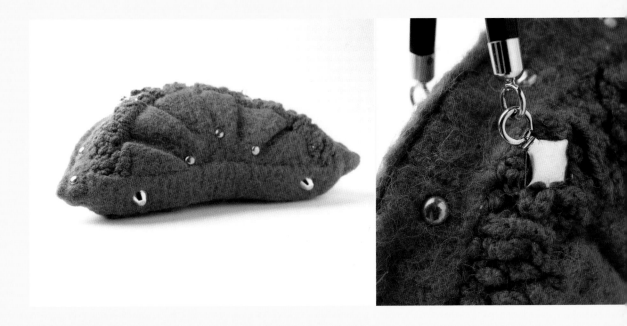

BLUE SPRUCE TOTE

Just as evergreen foliage takes on a special prominence when autumn leaves fall from the trees, this tote can be an important fall fashion statement. It's knit in a striking but uncomplicated cable pattern you're sure to enjoy, even if you've never worked cables before. Reinforced with tabs beneath the handles and a sturdy lining, this cotton classic will accompany you on shopping trips year-round.

SKILL LEVEL
Intermediate

FINISHED MEASUREMENTS
Length: 9 1/2"/24cm
Width: 9 1/2"/24cm
Depth: 2"/5cm

YARN
1 hank of S.R. Kertzer Butterfly Super 10 (100% mercerized cotton yarn, 125g = approx 249 yd/230m per hank) in #3783 Cayman OR approximately 249 yd/230m DK-weight mercerized cotton yarn in teal

MATERIALS
- Size 9 U.S. (5.5mm) needles or size needed to obtain gauge
- Cable needle
- Stitch markers
- 1 package (4 pcs) BagWorks Silver Foot Brads, #A3116-SIL, OR pair of 1/2" (12mm) silver purse feet
- 2 packages Dritz's Bag Boutique 3/4" (1.9cm) Magnetic Snaps, Silver, #9840 OR two 3/4" (1.9cm) silver magnetic snaps
- 1 package (96 pcs) M&J Trimming Ss40 Dome Nailheads 4-Prong, silver, #04040-S OR 4 Ss40 4-prong silver dome nailheads
- 1 pair of Tall Poppy Craft Vinyl Handles, Dark Brown with Rings, 22" X 5/8"/56cm

X 1.6cm, #hl7 OR pair of 22" X 5/8"/56cm X 1.6cm vinyl handles with rings in dark brown
- 1 sheet of Tandy Leather Factory Bag Stiffener, #9072-00 OR 1 sheet of bag stiffener
- Tapestry needle
- 1/4 yd (23cm) lining fabric of your choice
- Sewing needle
- Cotton thread to match yarn
- 1/4 yd (23cm) lightweight interfacing

GAUGE
18 sts = 4"/10cm over St st
Always take time to check your gauge.

PATTERN NOTES
- The body is knit flat and side edges are seamed together, forming a tube. The base is picked up from the cast-on edge. At the top of the purse, a garter stitch hem is folded over and whip-stitched into place.
- A chart and written instructions for Honeycomb Cable Stitch pattern are provided. Choose the instruction method you prefer.
- For instructions on cutting out lining, see page 32.
- For instructions on whip-stitching, see page 34.

SPECIAL ABBREVIATIONS
3-st Right Purl Twist: Sl 2 sts

to cable needle and hold in back of work, k1, p2 from cn.
3-st Left Purl Twist: Sl 2 sts to cable needle and hold in front of work, k1, p2 from cn.
3-st Left Knit Twist: Sl 1 st to cable needle and hold in front of work, p2, k1 from cn.
3-st Right Knit Twist: Sl 1 st to cable needle and hold in back of work, p2, k1 from cn.
Rnd: Round.

STITCH PATTERN
Honeycomb Cable Stitch (over a multiple of 6 sts)
Rows 1 and 3 (RS): *P2, k2, p2; rep from * across.
Row 2 and all WS rows: Knit the knit sts, purl the purl sts.
Row 5: *3-st Right Purl Twist, 3-st Left Knit Twist; rep from * across.
Rows 7, 9, and 11: *K2, p2, k2; rep from * across.
Row 13: *3-st Left Purl Twist, 3-st Right Knit Twist; rep from * across.
Row 14: *K2, p2, k2; rep from * across.
Rep rows 1–14 for Honeycomb Stitch patt.

PURSE
Body (Make 1)
CO 108 stitches. Work Honeycomb Cable Stitch patt four times (56 rows). Work in garter stitch for 8 rows (hem). BO all sts on WS.

Base

From left edge of cast-on edge with RS facing, skip first 10 sts, then pick up 34 sts. Work in garter stitch for 20 rows (10 ridges). BO all sts.

Tabs (Make 4)

Row 1 (RS): *K1, p1; rep from * across to last st, k1.
Row 2: Purl the knit sts and knit the purl sts.
Rep row 2 for nine rows.
BO all 9 sts.

FINISHING AND ASSEMBLY

1. Block knitted fabric.
2. Weave in ends.
3. Cut out lining according to instructions on page 32.
4. Cut lightweight interfacing 1/4" (6mm) smaller than knitted fabric.
5. Cut cardboard stiffener to size of base of knitted fabric.
6. Glue stiffener to wrong side of base.
7. Mark places for purse feet and attach two feet to the bottom of purse.
8. Glue lightweight interfacing to wrong side of knitted fabric.
9. With right sides facing, seam side edges of body together, forming a tube.
10. Whipstitch base to knitted body around remaining three sides.
11. Fold tabs over handle rings and whipstitch with matching yarn to secure.
12. Add one nail head to center of each tab.
13. Mark places for handles and whipstitch tabs into place on outside of bag with sewing thread.
14. Sew fabric lining. Hem top edge of lining. Place lining inside of bag, whipstitch to edge of garter stitch hem.
15. Mark areas on garter stitch hem for magnetic snaps and secure in place, remembering that hem will be turned to inside of bag.
16. Fold garter stitch hem over lining. Whipstitch into place.

DESIGN TIP

If you are sewing-savvy, add leather trim to the bag opening. It will give the bag a classier look, as well as adding reinforcement.

STITCH CHART
Honeycomb Cable Stitch
(over a multiple of 6 sts)

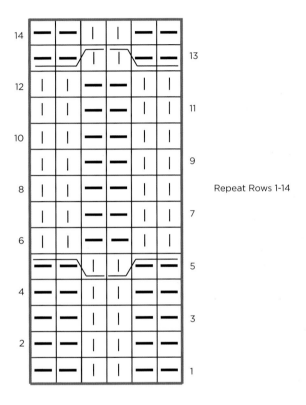

Repeat Rows 1-14

Legend

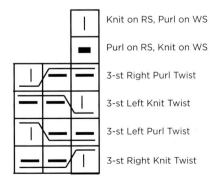

Knit on RS, Purl on WS

Purl on RS, Knit on WS

3-st Right Purl Twist

3-st Left Knit Twist

3-st Left Purl Twist

3-st Right Knit Twist

FLOWER POWER TOTE

Go wild making beautiful flowers in a deep, rich, autumnal red. Once you learn how to make knitted flowers, you'll soon be adorning many of your knitted pieces with floral masterpieces of your own creation. This bag is simple to line and to assemble, and its size makes it perfect for everyday use.

SKILL LEVEL
Intermediate

FINISHED MEASUREMENTS
Length: 11 1/2"/29cm
Width: 10 1/2"/27cm

YARN
1 hank of S.R. Kertzer Butterfly Super 10 (100% mercerized cotton yarn, 125g = approx 249/230m per hank) in #3424 crimson OR approximately 249 yd/230m DK-weight mercerized cotton yarn in dark red

MATERIALS
- Size 8 U.S. (5mm) straight needles and circular needle or size needed to obtain gauge
- 1 pair of Tall Poppy Craft vinyl adjustable strap handles, 22" to 24 5/8" long X 7/8"/56cm to 63 cm long X 1.2cm), #hl1, black, OR pair of 22" to 24 5/8" X 7/8" (56cm to 63cm X 1.2cm) black vinyl adjustable strap handles
- 1 set of Dritz Bag Boutique Magnetic Snaps (3/4"/1.9cm) in silver, #9840, OR 1 set of 3/4"/1.9cm silver magnetic snaps
- 1 package Dritz Innerfuse Double-Sided Stiff Fusible Interfacing, 14" X 18", Heavyweight #8306, OR other 14" X 18" (35.56cm X 45.72cm) heavyweight fusible interfacing
- 1 package Tandy Leather

Factory Double Cap Rivets, 3/8" cap, 5/16" post, 3/8" base, 100/pk, #1373-12 in nickel OR four medium double cap rivets, 3/8"(1cm) cap, 5/16" (.8cm) post, 3/8" (1cm) base in nickel
- Tapestry needle
- 1/2 yd (50cm) upholstery lining in tan
- Sewing needle and cotton thread to match the lining
- Measuring tape
- Iron

GAUGE
20 sts = 4"/10cm over garter st
Always take time to check your gauge.

PATTERN NOTES
- The stitch count in the Floral Lace Motif pattern will decrease from the first row to the last row.
- A chart and written instructions for Floral Lace Motif are provided. Choose the instruction method you prefer.
- For instructions on cutting out lining, see page 32.
- For instructions on whipstitching, see page 34.

SPECIAL ABBREVIATIONS
MB (Make Bobble): (K1, p1, k1, p1, k1, p1, k1) in the next st, making 7 sts from one; then pass the 6th, 5th, 4th, 3rd, 2nd, and 1st sts one at a time over the last stitch made.

K1-S10: Knit 1 st and sl back to LH needle. Slip ten stitches left of the slipped knit stitch, one at a time, off the LH needle. Yo2, knit the slipped knit st and slip it off LH needle.
Yo2: Yarn over twice

PATTERN STITCHES
Floral Lace Motif (over a multiple of 13 plus 2 extra)
Row 1 (WS): Purl.
Row 2: K2, * K1-S10, k2; rep from * to end. (27 sts)
Row 3: K1, *p2tog, drop first yo, (k1, p1, k1, p1, k1, p1) into second yo, p1; rep from * to last st, k1. (42 sts)
Row 4: K1, *(MB, k7); rep from * to last 9 sts, MB, k8.
Row 5: K2tog across. (21 sts)
Row 6: K2tog across to last three sts, k3tog. (10 sts)
Keep stitches on needle. Cut a length of yarn approximately 5 1/2"/14cm and thread through head of tapestry needle. Insert tapestry needle through first st on needle and through all remaining sts. Tighten to form a flower; seam sides together.

PURSE
Flower (Make 18 flowers)
CO 67 stitches. Work Flower Lace Motif.

Gusset
CO 10 sts. Work in garter st until 97 ridges are complete. BO all sts.

FINISHING AND ASSEMBLY

1. Weave in ends.
2. Place flowers according to placement diagram and join together at petals. Join nine flowers to form the front. Repeat with remaining 9 flowers for back.
3. Attach garter stitch borders by whipstitching around two sides and bottom of flowers for front and back.
4. To finish top edge of bag, pick up 102 sts around the top of bag (including two top petals of each flower and both garter stitch edge borders) with circular needle, forming a straight edge. Pm for beg of rnd; (k 1 rnd, p 1 rnd) four times. BO all sts.
5. Attach rivets to the attachment holes of purse handle tabs.
6. Mark positions for placement of handles and place tabs on wrong side (inside) of bag. Tack tab handles into place by whipstitching (see page 34).
7. Cut out lining according to directions on page 32, adding an extra 1"/2.54cm at top border edge.
8. Sew lining together.
9. Measure around the top edge of the lining. Cut a 1"/2.5cm wide strip of double-sided stiff fusible interfacing of the same length as the top edge.
10. Fold down top 1"/2.5cm edge of lining and insert double-sided stiff fusible interfacing between layers. Press with iron according to manufacturer's instructions.
11. Mark place for one magnetic snap at top center edge of lining and attach.
12. Whipstitch lining into bag, securing over tabs. (Optional: With sewing machine, straight stitch along top opening edge of bag.)

DESIGN TIP

Adding a braided cord will turn this tote into a sack bag.

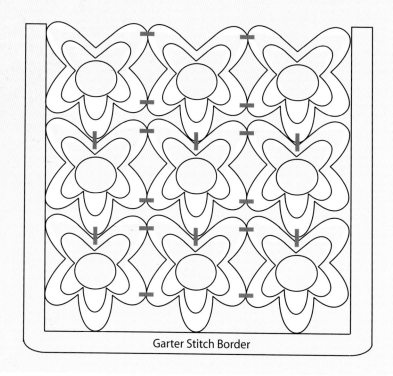

Garter Stitch Border

STITCH CHART
Floral Lace Motif
(multiple of 13 sts plus 2)

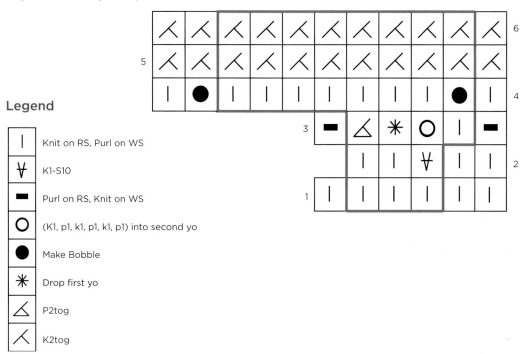

Legend

$\vert$	Knit on RS, Purl on WS
¥	K1-S10
▬	Purl on RS, Knit on WS
○	(K1, p1, k1, p1, k1, p1) into second yo
●	Make Bobble
✳	Drop first yo
△	P2tog
⋏	K2tog

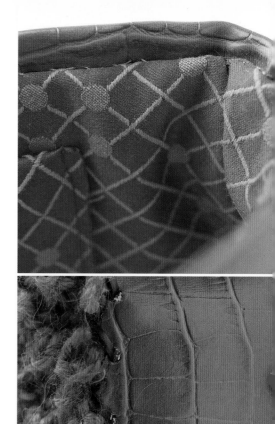

CLASSIC SATCHEL

The brilliant pumpkin color gives a surprising twist to this classic satchel-style handbag and makes it adaptable to many looks. Using simple knitting stitches—especially the time-tested bramble pattern—any advanced beginner will be able to craft this bag.

SKILL LEVEL
Easy

FINISHED MEASUREMENTS
Length: 7 1/2"/19cm
Width: 9"/23cm
Depth: 2"/5cm

YARN
1 hank of Schaefer Yarn Judith (100% prime alpaca, 4oz = approx 330 yd/302m per hank) in Margo Jones OR approximately 330 yd/302m DK-weight alpaca yarn in multi-orange

MATERIALS
- Size 9 U.S. (5.5mm) needles OR size needed to obtain gauge
- 1 package Dritz Innerfuse Double-Sided Stiff Fusible Interfacing, 14" X 18", Heavyweight #8306, OR 14" X 18" (35.56cm X 45.72cm) heavyweight double-sided stiff fusible interfacing
- 2 Muench Yarns Grayson-E 25" large rolled handles in amber OR two 25" (63.5cm) large rolled handles in orange
- 1 spool of Tandy Leather Factory's Ultra Vinyl Lace 3/32" X 100 yd, #5901-02, in dark brown OR 1 spool of 3/32" X 100 yd (.24cm X 99.4m) vinyl lace in dark brown
- 2 8 1/2" X 11" (21.6cm X 28cm) faux crocodile panels

in orange
- Tapestry needle
- Leather needles
- Scissors
- Pen
- Fabric glue
- Stitching awl, leather hole punch tool, or paper hole punch
- 1/4 yd (23cm) lining fabric of your choice
- 1/4 yd (23cm) lightweight interfacing
- Sewing needle and thread to match the lining
- Sewing machine (optional)

GAUGE
16 sts = 4"/10cm over St st with two strands of yarn held together.
Always take time to check your gauge.

PATTERN NOTES
- Two strands of yarn will be used throughout the pattern.
- Stitches before first marker and after last marker are increase stitches. Knit increase stitches on WS, purl increase stitches on the RS.
- A stitching awl, leather hole punch tool, or paper hole punch can be used to punch holes along the hem and the gusset.
- The leather pieces will be attached to the knitted fabric by vinyl lace thread using Freestyle Cross-Stitch. For instructions on Freestyle

Cross-Stitch, see page 36.
- For instructions on whip-stitching, see page 34.
- For instructions on cutting out lining, see page 32.

SPECIAL ABBREVIATIONS
Kp: Knitted piece(s).
P-inc: Purl into front, then into back of stitch.
P3tog: Purl 3 sts together.
P5tog: Purl 5 sts together.
PPSO: Pass p2tog st over p3tog st.

STITCH PATTERN
Bramble Stitch
Row 1 (RS): Purl across.
Row 2 (WS): *(K1, p1, k1) into next stitch, p3tog; rep from * to end.
Row 3: Purl across.
Row 4: *P3tog, (k1, p1, k1) into next stitch; repeat from * to end.
Rep rows 1–4 for Bramble Stitch patt.

BODY
(Make 2)
Unwind half the ball, cut yarn. Holding two strands of yarn together, CO 36 stitches. Work first two rows of Bramble Stitch patt.
Row 3 (RS): P-inc, pm after first st on RH needle, work row 3 of Bramble Stitch patt to last st, pm, p-inc, pm before last st.
Row 4 (WS): Work row 4 of Bramble Stitch patt.
Stitches placed before first

marker and stitches after the last marker are increase stitches. Purl increase stitches on the RS, knit increase stitches on the WS.

Continue increases on RS of work as established (work p-inc every row 3 of pattern) for 14 more rows (52 stitches). Whenever 4 sts appear outside of marker, incorporate these sts in Bramble Stitch patt and move marker. Work patt as established over 52 stitches until 32 rows (16 rows of bramble puffs) are formed. End on WS.

Decrease Rows:

Next row (RS): (P2tog, P3tog, ppso), purl to last 5 sts, p5 together.

Continue in patt and decrease on RS as established until 19 rows bramble puffs (38 rows total) are formed. End on RS. BO all sts on WS.

FINISHING AND ASSEMBLY

1. Weave in ends.
2. On low setting, press knit pieces on wrong side.
3. Cut lightweight interfacing 1/4" (6mm) smaller than knit pieces. Glue to wrong side of fabric and press down firmly. Set aside.
4. For the gusset, cut three pieces from the faux crocodile panel, each measuring 7" X 2"/18cm X 5.1cm.
5. For base gusset panel, punch three holes 1/2" (12mm) apart on both short sides, as shown in diagram. For both side gussets punch three holes on one side only. Punch an even number of holes 1/4" (6mm) apart on both long sides of the base and side gusset panels. (You will notice that the diagram shows two extra punched holes on top and bottom of gussets; continue by punching remaining holes 1/4" apart.)
6. Thread leather needle with vinyl thread and attach each side gusset to the base gusset using the freestyle cross-stitch (see page 36).
7. Cut lining with 1/4" (6mm) seam allowance for both body and joined gussets. Sew gusset and body lining pieces together, keeping top edge unsewn.
8. Cut one 7" X 2"/18cm X 5cm piece of double-sided stiff fusible interfacing for the base gusset.
9. For top edge of bag, cut two 10 1/2" X 1 1/2"/27cm X 4cm strips of faux crocodile. Seam, sewing both strips together to form a circular band.
10. Cut one 21" X 1 1/2"/54cm X 4cm strip of double-sided stiff fusible interfacing for the top edge of bag. Fuse the interfacing 1/4" (6mm) below top edge of lining, following manufacturer's directions. Fold lining over the interfacing and carefully iron on the lining to secure over interfacing.
11. Place top edge of faux crocodile over the purse and mark where the gusset will join, making sure it is even with the side gussets. Punch holes, referring to the diagram opposite. The top edge will be folded, overlapping both the exterior and the interior of bag.
12. Punch even number of holes 1/4" (6mm) apart on both long sides of the top edge.
13. Attach to bag by hand sewing, using the freestyle cross stitch (see page 36). Stitch through the top edge and knitted body of bag.
14. Glue the 7" X 2"/18cm X 5cm double-sided fusible interfacing to the interior base of bag. This will add extra support to the base.
15. Attach handles to front and back of bags with freestyle cross stitch.
16. Mark positions for placement of magnetic snaps. Attach magnetic snaps to lining.
17. Whipstitch lining to interior of bag.

DESIGN TIP

For greater ease, use deer lacing rather than vinyl lacing.

LEATHER ATTACHMENT

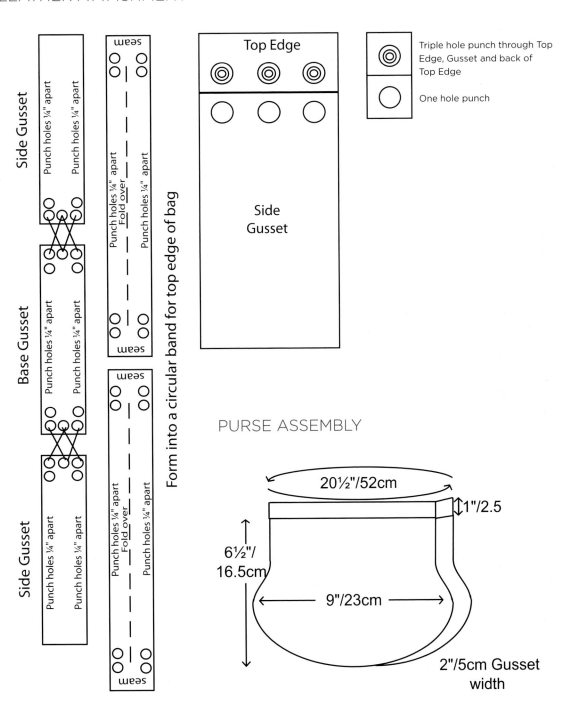

Side Gusset

Punch holes ¼" apart

Punch holes ¼" apart

Base Gusset

Punch holes ¼" apart

Punch holes ¼" apart

Side Gusset

Punch holes ¼" apart

Punch holes ¼" apart

seam

Punch holes ¼" apart
Fold over

Punch holes ¼" apart

seam

seam

Punch holes ¼" apart
Fold over

Punch holes ¼" apart

seam

Form into a circular band for top edge of bag

Top Edge

Side
Gusset

Triple hole punch through Top Edge, Gusset and back of Top Edge

One hole punch

PURSE ASSEMBLY

20½"/52cm

1"/2.5

6½"/
16.5cm

9"/23cm

2"/5cm Gusset
width

WINTER

MOCCASIN BAG

Here's an interpretation of the Native American pouch, this time in a deceptively simple bucket bag made of cabled knitting and soft deer-skin. The unique assembly technique—lacings threaded through hand-punched eyelets—forms the only decoration on this down-to-earth bag. Made of fine merino yarn and rustic suede, this bag has rugged good looks that will never go out of style.

SKILL LEVEL
Experienced

FINISHED MEASUREMENTS
Height: 8"/20cm
Diameter: 5"/13cm
Circumference: 15"/38cm

YARN
1 ball of Berroco Yarns Pure Merino (100% pure merino yarn, 1.75 oz/50g = approx 92 yd/85m per ball) in #8528 cocoon OR approximately 92 yd/85m medium-weight extra fine merino yarn in off-white

MATERIALS
- Size 9 U.S. (5.5mm) needles or size needed to obtain gauge
- Stitch markers
- Tapestry needle
- 2 (8 1/2" X 11") Tandy Leather Factory Cowhide Suede Trim Piece, #4040-30, in medium brown OR two 8 1/2" X 11" (21.6cm X 28cm) pieces of medium-brown cowhide suede trim
- 1 package (18 pcs) Bag-Works Additions 9.2mm Eyelets, #A3019-GLD, in gold OR nine 9.2mm gold eyelets
- 1 package (42 pc) BagWorks Additions 1/4" Eyelets, #A3022-GLD, in gold OR 42 1/4" (6mm) gold eyelets
- 1 package 3/16" x 54" Tandy Leather Deerskin Lace, #55003-00, in gold OR 3/16"

X 54" (.5 x 137cm) deerskin lace in gold
- 1 Tandy Leather Economy Rotary Punch #3220-00 OR other leather punch
- 1/4 yd (25cm) lining fabric of your choice
- Sewing thread (to match lining) and needle

GAUGE
18 sts = 4"/10cm over St st
Always take time to check your gauge.

PATTERN NOTES
- The entire bag is hand-sewn and is put together by threading deerskin suede lacing through eyelets.
- For instructions on cutting out lining, see page 32.
- For instructions on whip-stiching, see page 34.
- For instructions on working I-cord, see page 26.
- A chart and written instructions for Moccasin Cable Stitch are provided. Choose the instruction method you prefer. The stitch chart begins with a WS row. If you use the chart, take care to read WS rows (including Row 1) from left to right and RS rows from right to left.

SPECIAL ABBREVIATIONS
K2tbl: Knit two stitches together through back loops.
2-st Left Purl Twist: Sl 1 st to cable needle and hold in front

of work, p1, k1 from cn.
2-st Right Purl Twist: Sl 1 st to cable needle and hold in back of work, k1, p1 from cn.
Right Twist (RT): K2tog, leaving both sts on needle; insert RH needle between 2 sts, k first st again, slip both sts from needle.
Left Twist (LT): With RH needle behind LH needle, skip the first st and k second st tbl; insert RH needle into backs of both sts, k2tog tbl.
3-st Right Purl Cable: Sl 1 st to cable needle and hold in back of work, k2, p1 from cn.
3-st Left Purl Cable: Sl 2 sts to cable needle and hold in front of work, p1, k2 from cn.
4-st Right Cable: Sl 2 sts to cable needle and hold in back of work, k2, k2 from cn.

STITCH PATTERN
Moccasin Cable Stitch (over 26 sts)
Row 1 (WS): (K2, p1) twice, k5, p4, k5, (p1, k2) twice.
Row 2 (RS): P2, 2-st Left Purl Twist, 2-st Right Purl Twist, p5, 4-st Right Cable, p5, 2-st Left Purl Twist, 2-st Right Purl Twist, p2.
Row 3: Rep Row 1.
Row 4: Rep Row 2.
Row 5: K3, p2, k6, p4, k6, p2, k3.
Row 6: P3, RT, p5, 3-st Right Purl Cable, 3-st Left Purl Cable, p5, LT, p3.
Row 7: K3, p2, k5, p2, k2, p2, k5, p2, k3.

Row 8: P2, 2-st Right Purl Twist, 2-st Left Purl Twist, p3, 3-st Right Purl Cable, p2, 3-st Left Purl Cable, p3, 2-st Right Purl Twist, 2-st Left Purl Twist, p2.

Row 9: (K2, p1) twice, k3, p2, k4, p2, k3, (p1, k2) twice.

Row 10: (P2, k1) twice, p2, 3-st Right Purl Cable, p4, 3-st Left Purl Cable, (p2, k1) twice, p2.

Row 11: (K2, p1) twice, k2, p2, k1, p4, k1, p2, k2, (p1, k2) twice.

Row 12: P2, 2-st Left Purl Twist, 2-st Right Cable Twist, p1, 3-st Right Purl Cable, p1, 4-st Right Cable, p1, 3-st Left Purl Cable, p1, 2-st Left Purl Twist, 2-st Right Purl Twist, p2.

Row 13: K3, (p2, k2) twice, p4, (k2, p2) twice, k3.

Row 14: P3, RT, (p1, 3-st Right Purl Cable) twice, (3-st Left Purl Cable, p1) twice, LT, p3.

Row 15: K3, p2, k1, (p2, k2) three times, p2, k1, p2, k3.

Row 16: P3, RT, 3-st Right Purl Cable, p1, 3-st Right Purl Cable, p2, 3-st Left Purl Cable, p1, 3-st Left Purl Cable, LT, p3.

Row 17: K5, p2, k2, p2, k4, p2, k2, p2, k5.

Row 18: P4, 3-st Right Purl Cable, p1, 3-st Right Purl Cable, p4, 3-st Left Purl Cable, p1, 3-st Left Purl Cable, p4.

Row 19: K3, p2, (k4, p2) three times, k3.

Row 20: P2, 2-st Right Purl Twist, 2-st Left Purl Twist, p3, 3-st Left Purl Cable, p2, 3-st Right Purl Cable, p3, 2-st Right Purl Twist, 2-st Left Purl Twist, p2.

Row 21: (K2, p1) twice, k4, p2, k2, p2, k4, (p1, k2) twice.

Row 22: (P2, k1) twice, p4, 3-st Left Purl Cable, 3-st Right Purl Cable, p4, (k1, p2) twice.

Rep Rows 1–22 for Moccasin Cable Stitch patt.

PURSE

Body

CO 26 sts. Work from Moccasin Cable Stitch patt or chart until piece measures 15 1/2"/39cm from beginning. BO all sts on WS.

I-Cord

CO 4 sts. Work I-cord for 28"/71cm. BO all sts.

FINISHING AND ASSEMBLY

1. Weave in ends.
2. Seam the two suede trim pieces together along the 8 1/2"/21.6cm sides
3. From joined suede trim pieces, cut two 3" X 15"/7.6cm X 38cm suede strips for top and bottom of body.
4. Cut one 5"/12.7cm diameter suede circle for base.
5. Cut one 10" X 1"/25cm X 2.5cm strip for swivel hook handle.
6. Cut one 3" X 1"/7.6cm X 2.5cm tab for I-cord holder.
7. Punch small holes in suede strip and base according to Pre-Assembly diagram. Be sure that 37 small holes

in suede circle match holes on suede strip for bottom of body.

8. Punch holes for medium and large eyelets in suede strips for bottom and top of body as shown in pre-assembly diagram. **Note: Do not punch holes in knitted cable panel.**
9. Attach knitted cable panel to suede pieces by placing corresponding eyelet through knitted panel and through hole in suede strips. Refer to placement diagram.
10. Using the body made in step 9 as a pattern guide, fold over 1"/ 2.5cm from top. Cut a body lining, adding a 1/4" (6mm) seam allowance. Sew sides of lining together to form a circular band.
11. Using the base cut in step 4 as a pattern guide, cut a base lining, adding a 1/4" (6mm) seam allowance around diameter. Sew base lining to bottom of body lining, creating a cylinder.
12. Hammer eyelets down according to manufacturer's instructions. Continue attaching knitted cable panel to top and bottom suede strips.
13. Attach large eyelets to top suede trim according to placement diagram (14 large eyelets). Overlap side seams and join sides by

inserting medium eyelets through both layers of suede. Circular bands on suede strips are made. Whipstitch sides of knitted cable panel together to form a complete circular band.

14. Thread tapestry needle with suede lacing and weave tightly through bottom of body and circular base.

15. Place lining inside bag. Fold 1"/2.5cm of suede from top of bag over lining edge, matching large eyelets around top edge. Whipstich in place.

16. Create handle with 10"/25cm strip by punching hole as shown in pre-assembly diagram. Fold 1"/2.5cm over swivel hook D-ring on each side of handle and secure with large eyelet.

17. On top suede trim, weave I-cord through front and back of large eyelets, starting and ending through the same eyelet. Pull to front.

18. Seam I-cord tab together to form a circular ring and seam through center. Pull I-cord through each hole in I-Cord tab.

19. Make a knot 3"/7.6cm from each end of I-cord to secure.

20. Hook swivel hooks into large eyelets on opposite sides of bag.

DESIGN TIP

If you prefer not to use eyelets to join the suede trims, try joining trims using a sewing machine with a Teflon foot. Hand-sewers can easily sew the suede together using a needle adapted for leather.

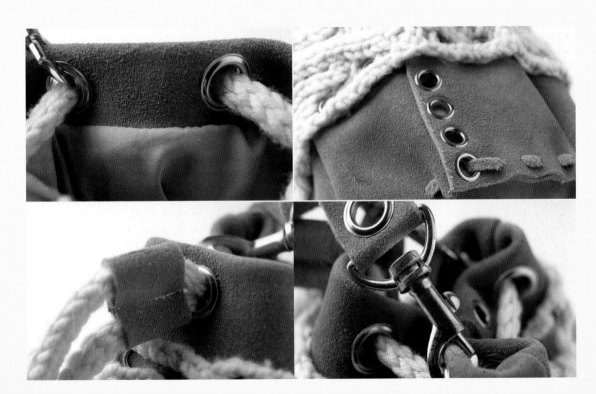

STITCH CHART
Moccasin Cable Stitch
(over 26 sts)

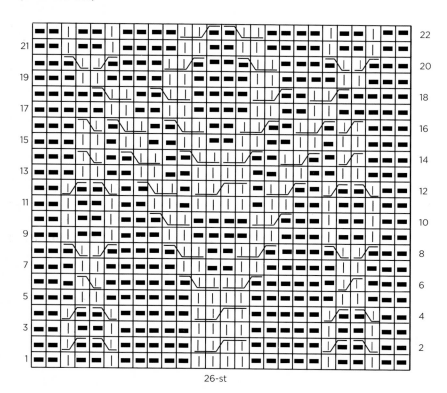

26-st

Legend

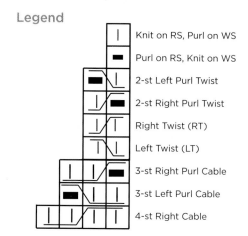

	Knit on RS, Purl on WS
	Purl on RS, Knit on WS
	2-st Left Purl Twist
	2-st Right Purl Twist
	Right Twist (RT)
	Left Twist (LT)
	3-st Right Purl Cable
	3-st Left Purl Cable
	4-st Right Cable

PRE-ASSEMBLY: HOLE PUNCH DIAGRAM

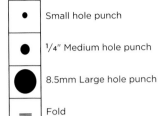

- • Small hole punch
- ● ¼″ Medium hole punch
- ⬤ 8.5mm Large hole punch
- = Fold

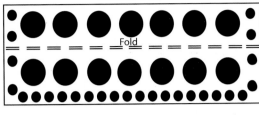

Suede trim

Cable

Suede trim
37 small hole punches

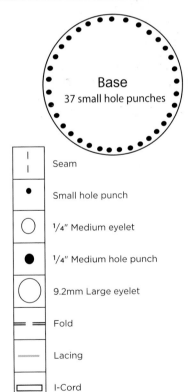

Base
37 small hole punches

PURSE ASSEMBLY

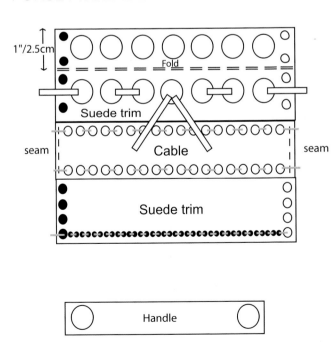

1″/2.5cm

Fold

Suede trim

seam   Cable   seam

Suede trim

Handle

- | | Seam
- • Small hole punch
- ◯ ¼″ Medium eyelet
- ● ¼″ Medium hole punch
- ◯ 9.2mm Large eyelet
- = Fold
- — Lacing
- ▭ I-Cord

RED DIAMOND CLUTCH

Brighten a winter day with this small but striking red clutch. This retro-looking design is knit in a twist-stitch pattern out of a rayon-blend yarn that's silky yet sturdy. The tortoiseshell purse frame lends a classic touch. This bag looks like something you paid serious money for in a vintage clothing store—but you'll know you made it yourself with only one skein of yarn.

SKILL LEVEL
Easy

FINISHED MEASUREMENTS
Length: 5"/12.7cm
Width: 5"/12.7cm
Depth: 1 1/2"/3.8cm

YARN
1 hank Berroco Yarns Softwist (41% wool/59% rayon yarn, 1 3/4 oz/50g = approx 100 yd/92m) in #9455 Cool Red OR approximately 100 yd/92m medium-weight wool/rayon blend yarn in red

MATERIALS
• Size 8 U.S. (5mm) needles or size needed to obtain gauge
• Tapestry needle
• Stitch markers
• 1 Lacis 5" Retro Vintage Lucite Purse Frame, #LD60, in tortoise, OR other 5" (12.7cm) Lucite purse frame in tortoise
• 1/4 yd (25cm) lightweight interfacing
• 1/4 yd (25cm) lining fabric of your choice
• 12 beads (6mm) in gold
• Fabric glue
• Double-stiff fusible interfacing (optional)
• Sewing needle and thread to match the lining

GAUGE
20 sts and 28 rows = 4"/10cm over St st

Always take time to check your gauge.

PATTERN NOTES
• Charts and written instructions are provided for Diamond Twist Stitch patt and Diamond Gusset Stitch patt. Choose the instruction method you prefer.
• The body is knit flat on straight needles. Near the base, 8 sts are cast on at each end to form gussets.
• For instructions on cutting out lining, see page 32.
• For instructions on whip-stitching, see page 34.

SPECIAL ABBREVIATIONS
Sm: Slip marker.
LT: With RH needle behind LH needle, skip the first st and k the second st tbl; insert RH needle into backs of both sts, k2tog tbl.
RT: K2tog, leaving both sts on needle; insert RH needle between 2 sts, k first st again, then slip both sts from needle.

STITCH PATTERNS
Diamond Twist Stitch (Chart A)
(over a multiple of 12 sts plus 2)
Row 1 (RS): K1, *LT, k2, RT; rep from * to last st, k1.
Row 2 and all other WS rows: Purl.
Row 3: K2, *LT, RT, k2; rep from * to end.

Row 5: K3, *LT, k4; rep from * to last 3 sts, k3.
Row 7: K2, *RT, LT, k2; rep from * to end.
Row 9: K1, *RT, k2, LT; rep from * to last st, k1.
Row 11: K6, *RT, k4; rep from * to last 6 sts, k6.
Row 12: Purl.
Rep rows 1–12 for Diamond Twist Stitch patt.

Diamond Gusset Stitch (Chart B)
(over 8 sts)
Row 1 (RS): K3, RT, k3.
Row 2 and all other WS rows: Purl.
Row 3: K2, RT, LT, k2.
Row 5: K1, RT, k2, LT, k1.
Row 7: LT, k4, LT.
Row 9: K1, LT, k2, RT, k1.
Row 11: K2, LT, RT, k2.
Row 12: Purl.
Rep rows 1–2 for Diamond Gusset Stitch patt.

Seed Stitch
(over even number of sts)
Row 1: *K1, p1; rep from * across.
Row 2: P the k sts and k the p sts.
Rep Row 2 for Seed St.

PURSE
CO 30 sts. Beg Diamond Twist Stitch patt, keeping two sts at beg and end of row in Seed Stitch. Work as established until the piece measures 5"/12.7cm from beg; end on WS. Work in Seed st over 30

sts for seven rows. End on RS. **Next row (WS):** CO 8 sts, p eight CO sts, pm, work remaining sts in Seed Stitch. (38 sts) **Next row (RS):** CO 8 sts, work 8 CO sts in Diamond Gusset Stitch, pm, work 2 sts in Seed Stitch, pm, work 26 sts in Diamond Twist Stitch beg from Row 1 of Diamond Twist Stitch, pm, work 2 sts in Seed Stitch, pm, work 8 sts in Diamond Gusset Stitch beg from Row 1 of patt. Work even, foll patts, until second Diamond Twist Stitch patt measures 5"/12.7cm from end of seed stitch patt. BO all sts on WS.

FINISHING AND ASSEMBLY

1. Weave in ends.

2. Block knitted fabric.
3. Cut lining according to instructions on page 32.
4. Cut lightweight interfacing to size of knitted fabric; trim 1/4" (6mm) from all edges.
5. Glue lightweight interfacing to wrong side of knitted fabric. (Optional: For extra support, measure the base, then cut and glue double-stiff fusible interfacing to the base.)
6. Whipstitch sides of knitted fabric (see page 34).
7. Sew lining and whipstitch lining to knitted purse.
8. Slip knitted purse into frame opening. This operation may require the use of a needle or flat toothpick.

9. Thread sewing needle with red thread. Position bead on right side of frame attachment hole. On wrong side of frame attachment hole, poke needle through hole to front of work and slip needle through bead. Poke needle through the same frame attachment hole. Repeat several times to secure. Knot thread on wrong side of frame. Repeat for remaining 11 frame attachment holes.

DESIGN TIP

If you use invisible thread when attaching the frame to the knitted bag, your sewing will be a lot less noticeable.

STITCH CHART A
Diamond Twist Stitch
(over a multiple of 12 sts plus 2 extra)

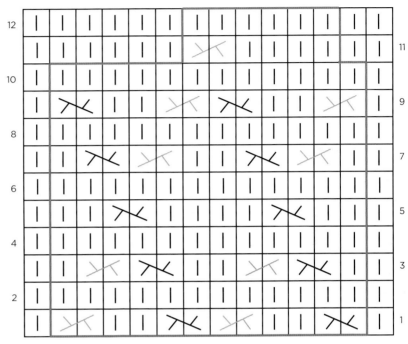

STITCH CHART B
(Diamond Gusset Stitch) (over 8 sts)

Legend for Charts A and B

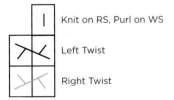

	Knit on RS, Purl on WS
	Left Twist
	Right Twist

BLUE CRESCENT

Light up a special evening with this silky clutch, the electric color of the deep blue winter sky just before sunset. This brilliant shade is perfect for holiday festivities and other special winter occasions. Lined in satin, the purse is knit in a simple scallop stitch and finished with a unique vintage-style frame.

SKILL LEVEL
Intermediate

FINISHED MEASUREMENTS
Height 5"/13cm
Width: 10"/25cm

YARN
1 hank of Tilli Tomas Simply Heaven (100% spun silk, 100g = 120 yd/110m per hank) in sapphire OR 120 yd/110m bulky-weight silk yarn in sapphire blue

MATERIALS
- Size 10 U.S. (6mm) needles or size needed to obtain gauge
- Spare needle in the same size as needles used for project OR a large cable needle
- 1 Sunbelt Fashion Classic/ Vintage Purse Frame, 3" X 6 1/2", SKU: SFPF-C38[S], in silver OR other 3" X 6 1/2" (8cm X 16.5cm) classic/vintage purse frame in silver
- 1/4 yd (25cm) lining fabric of your choice
- Sewing needle and cotton thread to match the lining
- Tapestry needle

GAUGE
16 sts = 4"/10cm over St st
Always take time to check your gauge.

PATTERN NOTES
- The stitch count will decrease from row 1 to row 3 of the Scallop Lace Stitch patt.
- Each body contains three scallop rows.
- Two scallops will be overlapped and joined to the previous scallop by 3-needle overlapping.
- A chart and written instructions for Scallop Lace Stitch Pattern are provided. Choose the instruction method you prefer.
- For instructions on whip-stiching, see page 34.
- For instructions on cutting out lining, see page 32.

SPECIAL ABBREVIATIONS
Yo2: Yarn over twice.
K1-S9: K 1 st and sl back to LH needle. Slip nine sts left of the slipped k st, one at a time, off the LH needle. Yo2, knit the slipped k st, and slip it off LH needle.
3-needle overlapping: * Hold spare needle and working needle parallel, with points facing to the right. Insert the RH needle knitwise into the first st on both needles. Knit both sts together. Repeat from * to end of row.

STITCH PATTERNS
Stockinette Stitch
Row 1 (RS): Knit.
Row 2 (WS): Purl.
Rep rows 1–2 for Stockinette Stitch.

Scallop Lace Stitch (over a multiple of 12 sts plus 2 extra)
Row 1 (WS): Purl.
Row 2: K2, * K1-S9, k2; rep from * to end.
Row 3: K1, *p2tog, drop first yo, (k1, p1, k1, p1, k1) into second yo, p1; rep from * to last st, k1.
Work rows 1–3 once for Scallop Lace Stitch patt.

PURSE
Front and Back (Make 2)
Base Level
CO 62 sts. Work rows 1–3 of Scallop Lace Stitch patt once (37 stitches). Work St st for 8 rows. End on WS. Keep 37 sts on needle. Cut yarn.

Second Level
CO 62 sts using spare needle. Work rows 1–3 of Scallop Stitch patt once (37 stitches).
Row 4: With RS facing, hold this scallop in front of the base-level scallops and work 3-needle overlapping over all 37 stitches. Turn. Purl next row. Work St st for 6 rows. End on WS. Keep 37 stitches on needle. Cut yarn.

Third Level
CO 62 sts on spare needle. Work rows 1–3 of Scallop Stitch patt once (37 stitches).
Row 4: With RS facing, hold

STITCH CHART
Scallop Lace Stitch
(multiple of 12 sts plus 2)

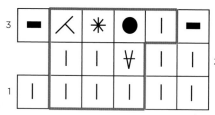

2 Work Rows 1-3 once

Legend

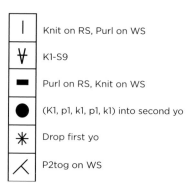

	Knit on RS, Purl on WS
⅄	K1-S9
▬	Purl on RS, Knit on WS
●	(K1, p1, k1, p1, k1) into second yo
✳	Drop first yo
⋏	P2tog on WS

---

this scallop in front of the second-level scallops and work 3-needle overlapping over all 37 stitches. Turn. Purl next row. Knit next row. BO all 37 stitches. Cut yarn.

FINISHING AND ASSEMBLY

1. Weave in ends.
2. Block knitted fabric.
3. Cut out lining according to instructions on page 32.
4. Whipstitch sides of knitted fabric together (see page 34).
5. Attach silver frame to knitted fabric through attachment holes using sewing thread.
6. Sew sides of lining and attach to inside of bag.

7. With matching thread, sew down scallop edges.

DESIGN TIP
Adding a silver chain will turn this clutch into a mini shoulder bag.

LES FLEURS

Brighten a winter night with this small but exquisite cigar-box-shaped bag. Super easy to make, it's knit in basic stockinette stitch that is then felted and cut to shape. A perfect first knitting project, this bag is embellished with embroidery and beading and finished with a golden clasp that opens to reveal a soft, bright-red interior.

SKILL LEVEL
Beginner

FINISHED MEASUREMENTS
Height: 2 1/2"/6cm (excluding handle)
Width: 8"/20cm
Depth: 5"/12cm

YARN
1 skein of Brown Sheep Nature Spun (100% wool yarn, 3.5 oz/100g = approx 245 yd/224m per skein) in #601 Pepper or approximately 245 yd/224m medium-weight wool yarn in black

MATERIALS
- Size 9 U.S. (5.5mm) needles or size needed to obtain gauge
- Tapestry needle
- Sewing needle
- 1 Ghee's 12" Abaca Rope Handbag Handle, #bacaRope in red or other 12" (31cm) rope handbag handle in red
- 1 9" X 12" (23cm X 31cm) sheet of Kunin Rainbow Felt in black or other 9" X 12" (23cm X 31cm) sheet of felt in black
- 1 skein DMC Pearl Cotton size 5 (100% cotton, 27.3 yd/25m) in #321red or approximately 27.3 yd/25m size 5 cotton embroidery thread in red
- 1 skein DMC Pearl Cotton size 5 (100% cotton, 27.3 yd/25m) in #900 DK burnt orange or approximately 27.3 yd/25m Size 5 cotton embroidery thread in dark burnt orange
- 9 6mm rhinestones
- 1 piece of cardboard, 8 1/2" X 11" (21.6cm X 28cm)
- 1/4 yd (23cm) lightweight batting
- 1/2 yd (50cm) lining fabric of your choice
- Fabric glue
- Chalk or crayon to mark the handle and lock positions
- Embroidery scissors
- 1 wooden cigar box, approx 5" X 8" X 1 1/2"/12 X 20 X 4cm

GAUGE
16 sts and 20 rows = 4"/10cm over St st
Always take time to check your gauge.

PATTERN NOTES
- The size of the knitted fabric is dictated by the size of the cigar box. If you use a cigar box larger than the one specified here, cast on more stitches and knit more rows to make a larger fabric.
- The knitted fabric will be felted, traced, cut, and embellished. The narrow-side edge strip will be joined with the top of the lid strip with buttonhole stitch. Then the fabric will be glued to the box.
- For instructions on Lazy Daisy Stitch, see page 36.
- For instructions on Chain Stitch, see page 35.
- For instructions on Buttonhole Stitch, see page 34.
- For felting instructions, see page 30.
- For instructions on cutting out lining, see page 32.
- For instructions on whip-stitching, see page34.

STITCH PATTERN
Stockinette Stitch
Row 1 (RS): Knit.
Row 2 (WS): Purl.
Rep rows 1–2 for Stockinette Stitch.

PURSE
Body and Top
CO 60 sts. Work in St st for 7"/17.5cm. BO all sts.

Edge
CO 120 sts. Work in St st for 5 1/2"/14cm. BO all sts.

FELTING
Refer to felting instructions on page on page 30. Allow fabric to air dry completely.

FINISHING AND ASSEMBLY
Cutting the Felt
1. For purse lid (A in diagram), cut one piece of knitted felt 8" x 5"/20cm X 12.6cm or size to match the top of your box lid.
2. For narrow edge of lid (B), cut one strip of knitted felt

26 1/2" X 1"/67cm X 2.5cm or size to fit around outside edge of top lid.

3. For wide edge of purse bottom (C), cut one strip of knitted felt 26 1/2" X 1 1/2"/67cm X 3.7cm or size to fit around outside edge of bottom lid.

4. For bottom base (D), trace knitted felt for top lid (A) onto store-bought felt and cut.

Attaching Lining to Cigar Box

1. Measure interior of top lid of box and cut out lining to cover both interior and 1/4" (6mm) across exterior lid. Repeat for interior base lining of cigar box. Glue both linings to inside of box.

2. Place bottom of cigar box on top of paper, trace around twice. Cut and use as template for cutting cardboard. Cut out cardboard and use to trace over batting and lining. Cut out lining, leaving an extra 1/4" (6mm) seam allowance to overlap exterior edge. Glue batting to cardboard. Lay batting facedown on top of wrong side of lining, folding lining edges over cardboard, and secure with glue. Repeat process for inside of box bottom.

Decorating the Knitted Felt

1. Thread floss onto tapestry needle. Refer to decoration diagram for placement of flowers.

2. Start by embroidering the top lid cover, narrow strip, and wide strip. (Do not decorate bottom base cover.)

3. The top lid cover will have 9 lazy daisy flowers.

4. The narrow strip for side edge of lid will alternate orange and red four-petal chain flowers, nine of each color.

5. The wide strip for the bottom body of purse will have sparse orange and red chain stitches.

6. Glue a rhinestone to the middle of each flower on top lid cover. (Refer to decoration diagram on following page.)

Attaching the Knitted Felt to the Box

1. Remove front lock and hardware, if any, from cigar box.

2. Attach top lid cover to narrow strip along long edge with buttonhole stitch (see page 34). Stitch short ends of narrow strip together.

3. Attach bottom store-bought felt base cover to wide strip along long edge with buttonhole stitch. Stitch short ends of wide strip together.

4. Mark place on top lid cover where handle should rest. Make a small incision in the felted fabric with embroidery scissors.

5. Dab glue to wrong side of top lid cover and attach to top lid of box. Be sure to overlap any lining extending over lid. Allow to dry completely.

6. Repeat step 5 for bottom base cover.

Adding Hardware

1. Slip handle into marked area.

2. Pinch felt over handle ends and whipstitch to secure.

3. Mark place where lock should rest.

4. Screw lock into place through felt and box.

DESIGN TIP

If you want to reinforce the handles, adding handle clamps will provide the extra support needed.

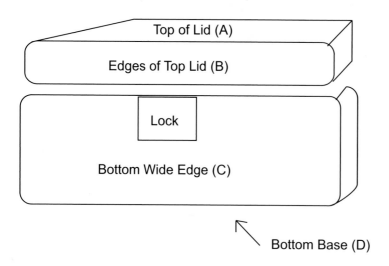

Top of Lid (A)

Edges of Top Lid (B)

Lock

Bottom Wide Edge (C)

Bottom Base (D)

DECORATION DIAGRAM

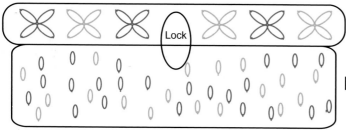

Side Edges of Lid

Lock

Bottom Body of Box

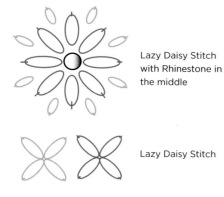

Lazy Daisy Stitch
with Rhinestone in
the middle

Lazy Daisy Stitch

Scattered Chain Stitch

Top of Lid

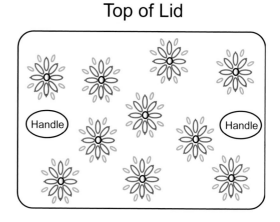

Handle   Handle

CABLED SATCHEL

Designed with both front and back pockets, this winter-white satchel will hold it all. It's knit with several different cable patterns and trimmed with leather, and it closes with a big leather clasp. This is the perfect fashion accessory for women who need a stylish, roomy bag.

SKILL LEVEL
Experienced

FINISHED MEASUREMENTS
Height: 9 1/2"/24cm
Width: 11 1/2"/29cm
Depth: 5"/12.7cm

YARN
1 skein of Caron Yarns Perfect Match (100% acrylic yarn, 7 oz/198g = approx 355yd/325m per skein) in #7775 cream OR approximately 355 yd/325m medium weight acrylic yarn in off-white

MATERIALS
- Size 8 U.S. (5mm) needles or size needed to obtain gauge
- Cable needle or spare needle
- Stitch markers
- 1 Ghee's 7" 900 Series tubular frame, #Tubular 907, OR other 7"/18cm tubular frame
- 1 pair Dritz Bag Boutique Vinyl Purse Handles, #9938, in black OR 1 pair black vinyl purse handles with rings
- 4 11/16" X 7/8" Tandy Leather Factory Oval Antique Bag Clasps, #1289-02, in nickel OR 4 11/16" X 7/8"/3cm X 2cm antique nickel oval bag clasps
- 2 Tandy Leather Factory Premium Leather Trim Pieces 8 1/2" X 11" (21.5cm X 28cm), #4040-60, in black OR 2 8 1/2" X 11" (21.5cm X 28cm) leather trim pieces

in black
- 1 package Tandy Leather Factory Double Cap Rivets, 3/8" cap, 5/16" post, 3/8" base, 100/pk, #1373-12, in nickel OR eight medium double cap rivets, 3/8"(1cm) cap, 5/16" (.8cm) post, 3/8" (1cm) base, in nickel
- 1 package Dritz Innerfuse Double-Sided Stiff Fusible Interfacing, 14" X 18", Heavy-weight #8306 OR other 14" X 18" (36cm X 46cm) heavy-weight double-sided stiff fusible interfacing
- 1/2 yd (50cm) lining fabric of your choice
- Tapestry needle
- Sewing needle and thread to match lining
- Fabric glue
- Hole punch

GAUGE
16 sts = 4"/10cm over St st
Always take time to check your gauge.

PATTERN NOTES
- Charts and written instructions for À La Mode Cable Stitch patt (Chart A), Gusset Stitch patt (Chart B), and Right and Left Pocket Stitch patterns (Charts C and D) are provided. Choose the instruction method you prefer.
- Two inset pockets are created on the second repeat of Chart A (row 9). Keep the stockinette stitch lining on the WS of the work. It will

be seamed to back of the work during finishing.
- The pocket flaps are worked and placed on stitch holders for later overlapping, as described below.
- For instructions on cutting out lining, see page 32.
- For instructions on whip-stitching, see page 34.

HOW TO OVERLAP
Overlap for knit stitches:
Insert the RH needle knitwise into the first st on the cable needle (or spare needle). Then insert the RH needle knitwise into the first st on the LH needle. K these 2 sts tog.

Overlap for purl and ptbl stitches: Insert the RH needle purlwise into the first st on the LH needle. Then insert the RH needle purlwise into the first st on the cable needle (or spare needle) as if to purl. P these 2 sts tog.

SPECIAL ABBREVIATIONS
16-st pleat B: Place Left Pocket Flap in back of work with its WS facing the RS of the work. Pleat the foll sts: p3, k2, p1 tbl, k2, p8.

16-st overlap A: Place Right Pocket Flap in back of work with its WS facing the RS of the work. Overlap the foll sts: p8, k2, p1 tbl, k2, p3.

3-st Left Twist: Sl 1 st to cable needle and hold in front of work, k2, k1 from cn.

3-st Right Twist: Sl 2 sts to cable needle and hold in back of work, k1, k2 from cn.

4-st Right Cable: Sl 2 sts to cable needle and hold in back of work, k2, k2 from cn.

4-st Left Cable: Sl 2 sts to cable needle and hold to front of work, k2, k2 from cn.

STITCH PATTERNS

À La Mode Cable Stitch
(over 53 sts)

Row 1 (RS): K1tbl, p2, k2, 4-st Right Cable, k2, (p2, k1 tbl, p2, k8) twice, p2, k1 tbl, p2, k2, 4-st Left Cable, k2, p2, k1 tbl.

Row 2 and all WS rows (WS): (P1 tbl, k2, p8, k2) four times, p1 tbl.

Row 3: K1 tbl, p2, (4-st Left Cable) twice, (p2, k1 tbl, p2, k8) twice, p2, k1 tbl, p2, (4-st Right Cable) twice, p2, k1 tbl.

Row 5: Rep row 1.

Row 7: Rep row 3.

Row 9: Rep row 1.

Row 11: K1 tbl, p2, k8, p2, k1 tbl, p2, k2, 4-st Right Cable, k2, p2, k1 tbl, p2, k2, 4-st Left Cable, k2, p2, k1 tbl, p2, k8, p2, k1 tbl.

Row 13: K1 tbl, p2, k8, p2, k1 tbl, p2, (4-st Right Cable) twice, p2, k1 tbl, p2, (4-st Left Cable) twice, p2, k1 tbl, p2, k8, p2, k1tbl.

Row 15: Rep row 11.

Row 17: Rep row 13.

Row 19: Rep row 11.

Rep 20: Rep row 2.

Rep rows 1–20 for À La Mode Cable Stitch patt.

À La Mode Cable Gusset Stitch
(over 18 sts)

Rows 1, 3, 5, 7, and 9 (RS): P2, k1 tbl, p2, k8, p2, k1 tbl, p2.

Row 2 and all WS Rows: K2, p1 tbl, k2, p8, k2, p1 tbl, k2.

Row 11: P2, k1 tbl, p2, k2, 4-st Right Cable, k2, p2, k1 tbl, p2.

Row 13: P2, k1 tbl, p2, (4-st Left Cable) twice, p2, k1 tbl, p2.

Row 15: Rep row 11.

Row 17: Rep row 13.

Row 19: Rep row 11.

Row 20: Rep row 2.

Rep rows 1–20 for À La Mode Cable Gusset Stitch patt.

Right Pocket Flap Stitch
(over 16 sts)

Row 1 (RS): 3-st Left Twist, k2, k1 tbl, p2, k8.

Rows 2 and 6 (WS): P8, k2, p1 tbl, k2, p3.

Row 3: K3, p2, k1 tbl, p2, k8.

Row 4: P8, yo, k2tog, p1 tbl, k2, p3.

Row 5: Rep row 1.

Row 7: Rep row 3.

Work rows 1–7 once for Right Pocket Flap Stitch patt.

Left Pocket Flap Stitch
(over 16 sts)

Row 1 (RS): K8, p2, k1 tbl, p2, 3-st Right Twist.

Rows 2 and 6 (WS): P3, k2, p1 tbl, k2, p8.

Row 3: K8, p2, k1 tbl, p2, k3.

Row 4: P3, k2, p1 tbl, k2, yo, p2tog, p6.

Row 5: Rep row 1

Row 7: Rep row 3.

Work rows 1–7 once for Left Pocket Flap Stitch patt.

POCKETS

Right Pocket Flap (Make 2)

CO 16 sts. Work Right Pocket Flap Stitch patt once. Do not BO. Leave sts on holder.

Left Pocket Flap (Make 2)

CO 16 sts. Work Left Pocket Stitch Flap patt once. Do not BO. Leave sts on stitch holder.

FRONT AND BACK BODY
(Make 2)

CO 53 stitches. Work À La Mode Cable Stitch patt (Chart A), completing rows 1–20 once, then rows 1–8 one more time.

Row 9: Work first 24 sts as in patt. Turn.

Making First Pocket

Next Row: Knit 16 sts. This row forms a turning ridge. Turn.

Next row (RS): Knit 16 sts. Turn.

Next row (WS): Purl 16 sts. Repeat last two rows (St st) until work measures 9"/23cm in length from turning row, ending on WS. Turn.

Continue row 9 (RS): Knit 16, work next 21 sts on LH needle in patt. Turn.

Making Second Pocket

Next Row: Knit 16 sts (turning ridge created). Turn.

STITCH CHART A
À La Mode Cable Stitch
(over 53 sts)

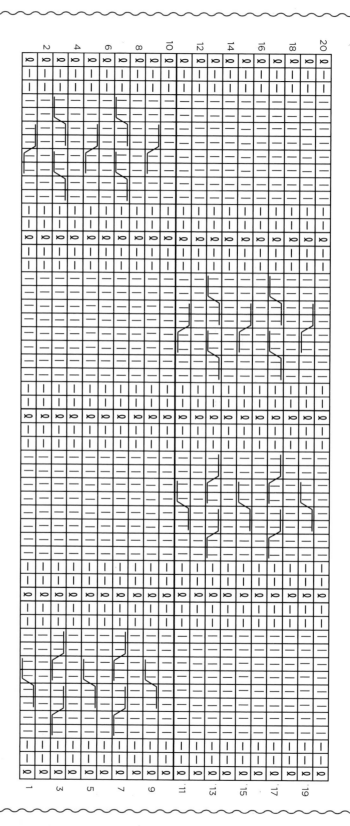

STITCH CHART B
À La Mode Cable Gusset Stitch
(over 18 sts)

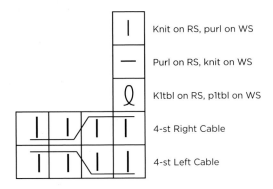

Legend for Charts A and B

|	Knit on RS, purl on WS
—	Purl on RS, knit on WS
Ω	K1tbl on RS, p1tbl on WS
	4-st Right Cable
	4-st Left Cable

Next row (RS): Knit 16 sts. Turn.

Next row (WS): Purl 16 sts. Repeat last two rows until work measures 9"/23cm from turning ridge, ending on WS.

Next row (RS): K 16, work remaining 8 sts on LH needle in patt. Row 9 completed.

Adding Pocket Flaps

Transfer stitches for Left and Right Pocket Flaps to a cable needle or spare needle.

Row 10: Work 8 sts, 16-st overlap B over Left Pocket Flap stitches, work next 5 sts in patt, 16-st overlap A over Right Pocket Flap stitches, work 8 sts.

Rows 11–13: Continue in patt.

Row 14: Decrease one st at the beg and end of this row and each foll row until 31 sts remain.

Next row: K the k sts, p the p sts.

Repeat the last row until the front body (excluding stockinette pockets) measures 9"/23cm. BO remaining 31 sts.

SIDE GUSSET

(Make 2)

CO 18 sts. Work À La Mode Cable Gusset Stitch patt (Chart B) until piece measures 9"/23cm from beginning. BO all sts.

FINISHING AND ASSEMBLY

1. Press wrong side of knitted fabric lightly with iron on low heat.
2. Cut and sew lining according to directions on page 32. Hem top edge of lining.
3. With right sides facing, seam sides of bag together, alternating gussets with front and back body pieces.
4. Weave in ends.
5. Cut out one 5" X 11 1/2"/13cm X 29cm piece of black leather for base.
6. Cut one 4 1/2" X 11"/11cm X 28cm piece of double-stiff fusible interfacing and glue to bottom of black leather base.
7. Whipstitch black leather base to sides of body, attaching on wrong side so that stitching is not visible.
8. Cut out 4 black leather tabs, each measuring 1" X 3"/2.5cm X 7.6cm, for attaching purse handles to bag.
9. Fold each tab over handle rings.
10. Punch holes where rivets will be placed (refer to diagram).
11. Attach tabs to bag with rivets, and hammer to secure in place.
12. Measure around top edge of bag. Cut a piece of black leather 5"/12.7cm wide X length of measured edge.
13. Whipstitch leather to top edge of bag on inside of knitted piece so that stitching is not visible.
14. Open tubular frame and place above wrong side of leather.
15. Fold leather over tubular frame and pull tightly over frame.
16. Glue just below whipstitched leather edge and press both edges of leather together snugly around tubular frame. (You may need to use tape or paperclips to hold the edges together.) Allow to dry completely.
17. Insert lining into bag and, using sharp needle, whipstitch top edge of lining over tubular leather edge.
18. Attach oval clasps to front pockets according to manufacturer's directions.

DESIGN TIP

If you use a sewing machine to attach the leather, be sure to use a stabilizer and/or a Teflon foot.

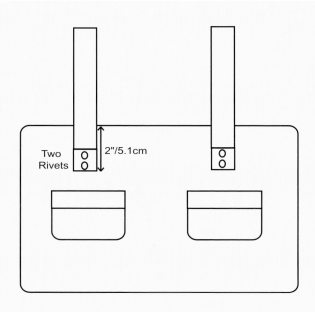

Two
Rivets

2"/5.1cm

STITCH CHART C
Right Pocket Flap Stitch
(over 16 sts)

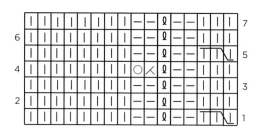

STITCH CHART D
Left Pocket Flap Stitch
(over 16 sts)

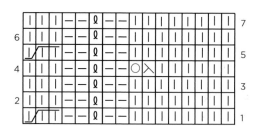

Legend for Charts C and D

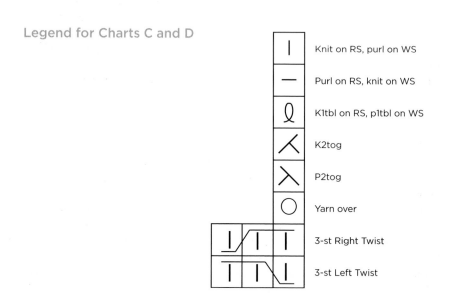

	Knit on RS, purl on WS
—	Purl on RS, knit on WS
Q	K1tbl on RS, p1tbl on WS
人	K2tog
人	P2tog
O	Yarn over
	3-st Right Twist
	3-st Left Twist

SUPPLIERS

If you cannot find the yarn or craft supplies you want at your local store, contact these wholesalers or visit their websites.

YARN

Berroco, Inc.
14 Elmdale Road
P.O. Box 367
Uxbridge, MA 01569
www.berroco.com

Brown Sheep Co., Inc.
100662 County Road 16
Mitchell, NE 69357
(800) 826-9136
www.brownsheep.com

Caron International
Customer Service
P.O. Box 222
Washington, NC 27889
www.caron.com

Coats & Clark
Consumer Services
P.O. Box 12229
Greenville, SC 29612-0229
(800) 648-1479
www.coatsandclark.com

Feza Yarns
453 Pepper Street, Unit 104
Monroe, CT 06468
(800) 684-3392
www.fezayarns.com

Lion Brand Yarns
135 Kero Road
Carlstadt, NJ 07072
(800) 258 YARN
www.lionbrand.com

Louet North America
808 Commerce Park Drive
Ogdensburg, NY 13669
In Canada:
3425 Hands Road
Prescott, ON KOE 1TO
www.louet.com

Patons
320 Livingstone Avenue
    South
Listowel, ON N4W 3H3
Canada
(888) 368-5401
www.patonsyarns.com

Rowan Yarns
Distributed by
Westminster Fibers
4 Townsend West, Unit 8
Nashua, NH 03063
(603) 886-5041

Schaefer Yarn Company
3514 Kelly's Corners Road
Interlaken, NY 14847
(607) 532-9452
www.schaeferyarn.com

Tilli Tomas
(617) 524 3330
www.tillitomas.com

Twilley's Yarn
Distributed by
S. R. Kertzer Limited
6060 Burnside Court, Unit 2
Mississauga, ON L5T 2T5
Canada
(800) 263-2354
www.kertzer.com

BEADS

Creativity Inc.
Blue Moon Beads and
    Westrim Crafts
7855 Hayvenhurst Avenue
Van Nuys, CA 91406
(800) 727-2727
www.creativityinc.com

BUCKLES AND PURSE HARDWARE

Bag Boutique and Dritz
Distributed by
Prym Consumer USA Inc.
P.O. Box 5028
Spartanburg, SC 29304
(800) 255-7796
www.dritz.com

BagWorks Inc.
Attn: Customer Service
3301-C South Cravens Road
Fort Worth, TX 76119
(800) 365-7423
www.bagworks.com

Ghee's
P.O. Box 4424
Shreveport, LA 71134
(318) 226-1701
www.ghees.com

Joyce Trimming, Inc.
109 W 38th St.
New York, NY 10018
(800) 719-7133
www.ejoyce.com

Lacis
3163 Adeline Street
Berkeley, CA 94703
(510) 843-7178
www.lacis.com

M&J Trimming
1008 Sixth Avenue
(between 37th and
38th Streets)
New York, NY 10018
(800) 9-MJTRIM
www.mjtrim.com

Muench Yarns, Inc.
1323 Scott Street
Petaluma, CA 94954-1135
(800) 733-9276
www.muenchyarns.com

Sunbelt Fashion
5037 Exposition Boulevard
Los Angeles, CA 90016
(800) 642-6587
www.sunbeltfashion.com

Tall Poppy Craft Products
(212) 813-3223
In Australia:
P.O. Box 391
Hurstville BC NSW 1481
Sydney, Australia
www.tallpoppycraft.com

Tandy Leather Factory, Inc.
3847 East Loop 820 South
Fort Worth, TX 76119
(800) 433-3201
www.tandyleatherfactory.com

INDEX